"From the first chapter on, this is a practical guide that shows residential real estate agents the process of how to create a sale to how to build a big business. Peter knows real estate! This book is like having a hotline to your mentor 24/7. As a professional coach and trainer, Peter's book is the hammer in my resource toolkit."

—**Dru Lee,** National Real Estate Coach

"Finally, a 'how-to' handbook for residential real estate agents. This should be on every agent's bookshelf to read and then reference often as they grow their business."

—**Stephen Cooley,** 15,000 Homes Sold
Charlotte, North Carolina

"I love this book and Peter has given a monumentally powerful tool for our industry. Strong work, my friend."

—**Dirk Mathews,** Oklahoma City Metro Real Estate Agent

PREP

PREP

PRACTICAL
REAL ESTATE
PRACTICES

A Handbook for Residential
Real Estate Agents

PETER LEVINSON

Stonebrook Publishing
Saint Louis, Missouri

A STONEBROOK PUBLISHING BOOK
©2023, Peter Levinson
This book was guided in development and
edited by Nancy L. Erickson, The Book Professor®
TheBookProfessor.com

Library of Congress Control Number: 2023916305

ISBN: 978-1-955711-31-9

stonebrookpublishing.net
PRINTED IN THE UNITED STATES OF AMERICA

"We don't do this because it's easy;
we do this because we *thought* it would be easy."
~Author Unknown

CONTENTS

PART 3: KEEP IT PROFESSIONAL

PART 4: PLAY NICE WITH OTHERS

PART 5: TIME AND MONEY

The purpose of this book is to guide residential real estate agents through easy-to-perform activities that will produce income. Whether you're a new agent, an experienced agent, or an agent who wants to be consistent in income-producing real estate activities, this book is for you.

INTRODUCTION

My wife, Tara Levinson, had been an agent since 2003, when I decided to venture into real estate in 2007. I'd been a regional marketing manager for a national retail store and covered multiple states. I typically traveled Monday through Friday every week and answered calls all weekend.

Tara, the growing real estate star at her brokerage, worked weekdays and every weekend to show houses, list houses, work open houses, etc. She was working on client files when she wasn't with a client. Unless I played chauffeur or open house companion, we didn't see each other much. That lifestyle came to a crash in 2007, at which time she made three times more than I did, and her star was only growing brighter. That realization led to me quitting my job and leaving behind the retail store world I'd worked in since I left the United States Marine Corps.

For a relationship reset, we went to Puerto Vallarta for a week to reconnect. When we got home, I focused on earning my real estate license. Once licensed, I joined the same brokerage where Tara worked. Because she was one of the top agents in her brokerage, she had her own office that overlooked one of our area's most prestigious golf courses. As I moved into her office, I quickly learned that I was in a new world—her world. For starters, she worked at her large, presidential-style desk while I set up shop at a six-foot-wide by two-foot-deep plastic folding table pushed against the wall, although I did have a pretty good chair.

This eventually became what I call my first lesson in real estate. You can have ego, or you can have money. You can seldom have both. The truth is that when you have ego, you can seldom have anything else. The bigger your ego is, the more it pushes everything else away. I had lived with a pretty big ego up to this point. However, I now needed to attract rather than push away. So goodbye ego, hello plastic executive office desk.

> You can have ego, or you can have money. You can seldom have both.

Now, the work began. I don't believe in reinventing the wheel. Improvements can be made to the wheel, but one must first see what others have done. Success leaves clues. My thought was that others had been selling real estate for decades. And though I was learning a lot from working with my wife, I wanted to see what else was out there and who else I could learn from.

As I sat at my desk, I began researching real estate books, trying to find how-tos. I discovered a multitude of books about theories, mindsets, and many over-the-top stories of real estate writers that said, to have success, you had to knock on a million doors a day, make a million phone calls, and write a million letters. Well, maybe not a million, but it felt like that. Who had time to do all that lead generating and still have time to work with clients? Or better yet, I was married with two teenage kids. I still had to live a life. I gave up being an absentee figure when I quit my job for a career in real estate. I certainly wasn't going to start giving all my time away again.

The way I looked at it, doing all that stuff was fine and good if I was looking for something that would give me results, but it wasn't sustainable. Sure, it would work initially for the budding real estate agent, but not if I was showing twenty properties a day, going on listing appointments, and performing general real estate income maintenance activities.

My other question was, *What would I say if I did these things?* My next question was, *How do I do an open house?* The more I researched, the more questions I had.

Of course, doing a certain amount of each of these activities is essential. But how could I draw upon the ultimate power of the Pareto Principle so that the words I used and the actions I took would create that 80 percent result with just 20 percent of the most critical work?

The one book I wanted but never found was one that would lead a new agent step by step to earn an income through practical actions. Most books were written to entice the agent into believing they'd be the next top agent, just as the author had achieved. There was little insight into how an agent can go from earning their real estate license to completing their first transaction. Maybe the authors believed the brokerage would help agents do that, so they didn't need to put that information in a book. But the truth is that very few brokerages do that.

> The one book I wanted but never found was one that would lead a new agent step by step to earn an income through practical steps.

Perhaps my time in the Marine Corps made me seek this instruction. In the Marine Corps, my primary job function was that of an aviation electrician, including communication/navigation equipment. No matter how many times I'd changed out a generator on an engine, I still took out the publication that walked me through the process step by step. Failure to do a job correctly could result in a plane crash and loss of life.

Real estate isn't life or death, but it's essential. It's often the single most significant investment a person will make. I wanted something like those aircraft publications for my daily real estate career.

This book is designed to be read in two ways: cover to cover and as a reference book. Many concepts, thought processes, etc., may be duplicated in some way, form, or fashion in each section. This isn't to fluff the book up or to add more pages; it's to ingrain the concepts, change your thought patterns, and get you to think differently. After reading it cover to cover, it's also to provide a way for you to go back and review sections to implement. When you pick an area you want to improve, you can work on that section without missing any concepts.

Success isn't sexy. Social media sites and online real estate coaches too often present a false narrative of what success looks like. Social media is designed to be attractive, to captivate the audience, and to have them craving and coming back for more. Success, on the other hand, is usually monotonous. Success means repeating basic systems and processes every day, every week, every month until the beginning of each new year, you stop and ask yourself, *Can I do it all again?* With repetition, you've executed your processes so often that they'll naturally produce results—as long as you continue the monotonous, repetitive tasks.

I will show you how to build and operate a successful real estate business. You'll build on those strategies, and over time, make the strategies and principles fit your business style. Now, let's get going.

THE BIG PROBLEM WE WILL SOLVE

The problem I discovered in 2007 hasn't changed in the fifteen-plus years I've worked in real estate. Many books teach great mindset strategies about overcoming client issues, setting up your day, and winning a listing (typically through a story). Other books reference building a team, structuring your showings, etc. But, until now, there's been no reference book for real estate agents that teaches the tasks and behaviors—the nitty gritty repeatable behaviors—necessary to become a successful, sustainable, and profitable real estate agent.

You're holding that book now.

Real estate schools teach the laws, the basic terms of the real estate industry, and a few scenarios so you don't get sued or lose your license. Surprisingly, very few schools (if any) go over contracts. I can't believe how many agents don't know anything about contracts, appraisals, negotiating offers, etc. To get a driver's license, you must demonstrate proficiency in driving an automobile. To get a real estate license, all you need to know is the law, like passing the written driver's test and saying, "Good luck, and don't kill anyone."

Real estate commissions rely on brokers to ensure their agents know how to conduct themselves. The advent of the internet, online training, and pursuit of the lowest possible split an agent pays to the brokerage hasn't increased actual knowledge. To train their agents, brokers rely increasingly on video training, web calls, etc. How much information do you think someone retains during these sessions? It's probably between 20 percent and 50 percent of the course if they're like me.

I'll tell you a secret, and don't judge me for it. When I have to take an online course where I'm listening to someone speak, I get super distracted. I always turn the video camera off and work on another project while listening to the course. I've been known to build a Lego project while taking a class. Building Legos is a side hobby of mine, part of my morning meditation, but that's a story for another time.

How This Book Solves the Problem

An aircraft maintenance publication takes a person through the process of replacing any component on an airplane step by step. Likewise, this book is designed to walk you through the various methods a real estate agent performs in their day-to-day activities, step by step. The book is divided into five sections, each with subsections for specific topics that fall within that section. The main areas are as follows:

1. Creating Business

This section will make it easy for agents to learn where to find business through open houses, your sphere of influence, for-sale-by-owner properties, expired listings, self-marketing, marketing your business, marketing your listings, farming (not the garden type), and social media platforms.

Yes, an agent can find any of the above topics online through subscription services, videos, etc., but this section puts it all in one place to quickly reference, making it easy to access when needed. If you have a team, you can hand them the book and tell your agent, support staff member, or virtual assistant what section to reference and what activities to execute.

2. I Have a Lead—Now What?

Have you asked yourself that question yet? If not, it may surprise you how often this question is asked. If not externally, it's undoubtedly requested internally. After getting a lead, whether a buyer, seller, or seller who also needs to buy, this section breaks down various scenarios a real estate agent has with clients. It includes things like working with seller leads, working with sellers after their property is listed for sale, sellers under contract, buyer leads, buyers under contract, sellers who are also buyers (working the transactions simultaneously), working internet leads, working with referrals, and working with leads that you've paid to get.

I've found very little information to guide agents through the systems and processes they need once they have a client's business. Without the real estate coach who challenged my wife early in our business, we would never have documented our systems and processes. Let me tell you, this was not an easy task to do. We worked our regular, long real estate schedule every day, and in the evening, we worked well into the night to write out our systems and processes to create a manual for our business. I don't know where we'd be today if we hadn't done that.

3. Keep It Professional

This section teaches you how to operate your business like a business. Please don't gloss over this part. Your level of professionalism will be a big part of your real estate business trajectory. Learn how to become a top-notch professional.

Having a real estate license doesn't mean you're a professional. Many people have driver's licenses, but very few can be labeled professional drivers. You must be above average if you want to set yourself apart from the industry averages. Set yourself apart from the part-time agents who got their real estate license because they "love looking at houses."

This section teaches you how to always be professional, to respect other agents, to know the real estate laws, to know the contracts and supporting documents, and most importantly, to know why you never, ever deviate.

4. Play Nice with Others

To have a long, successful real estate career, you must learn to play nice with others. You'll want to create long-lasting relationships and partnerships with other industry professionals such as lenders, inspectors, title companies, appraisers, etc.

Too often, real estate agents treat the other professionals who are part of the transaction as either cash machines that support their business or obstacles to earning a commission. Early on, I saw a need to partner with vendors to create working relationships that care for both the clients and my personal business.

Because of these professional relationships, when something needs to happen to take care of the client, the vendors and I partner to make it happen. I've never been held hostage by another real estate professional because I've never taken anything from them. We are partners, each doing our part to satisfy our clients' needs.

5. Time and Money

This section will show you how to protect your time and manage your money. You'll learn how to manage your time and your client's time and what it means to spend time on real estate. Too many agents think they're working on real estate when they're wasting everyone's time. This section highlights time management scripts and techniques, the differences between personal and professional time, and respecting the client's time.

Money is another essential part of working in real estate. I didn't get into real estate because I wanted to help people. If that were the case, I would have been a doctor. I also didn't get into real estate because I had a burning desire to help someone find their dream home. I got into real estate to make money. Our company mission statement is simple: We Sell Real Estate.

I want to teach you how to control your money so you don't live commission check to commission check. In this section, we talk about mythical, magical money, how to track your money, how to manage what you spend, and how to invest (in real estate).

In the final chapter, we discuss that you aren't the first real estate agent. Too often, agents forget that the wheel has already been invented, and they try to do this complicated job without help from others. That's another waste of your time. After you read this chapter, I hope that won't be you.

Now, let's dive in!

PART 1

CREATING BUSINESS

1

OPEN HOUSES

I'm going to make a big assumption right now and say that you, like the many real estate agents I know, had a vision of your life when you got your real estate license. As the old miner would say in a crusty, ragged voice, "There's gold in them darn hills!"

Maybe as you were working through the licensing process, you envisioned that your friends and family would hire you as their real estate agent. And in your story, maybe that happened. But I've met many a Rookie of the Year who completely vanished after their first year in the business. What happened in year two? They didn't know what to do after all their friends and family bought or sold a house. Here's a hard truth: the phone doesn't ring on its own.

> Business is created, not found.

So where do you get sustainable business—month after month and year after year? Business is created, not found. You cannot find business.

Let me give you a scenario. You're sitting at an open house. A couple walks in to view the property. You ask yourself, *Are they lost?* The answer is no, they aren't lost. They know exactly where they are and why they are there. You cannot find what isn't lost. Yet this is so many agents' attitude in every aspect of their real estate business.

Often, the way an agent greets visitors at an open house is the equivalent of, "Oh my gosh, I found you. Here's my card in case you get lost again. Now get in my car, and I'll show you houses from now on, so you'll never get lost again. Aren't you happy that I, that great real estate agent, found you?"

I'm going to pause this scenario here. Don't worry; you can pick it back up quickly.

My goal isn't to teach you to *find* business. I'll teach you to *create* business. Walt Disney didn't find Disney World; he created it. Elon Musk didn't find Tesla; he created it. Warren Buffet didn't find billions of dollars; he created them.

You will learn how to *create business*—to create income. No more hoping and dreaming that you'll find business like a dollar on the ground. You will create your dollars and lots of them. If you control your activities, you can influence your results.

Let's go back to the open house scenario. The couple isn't lost because they came to view that house that you marketed. You're there to sell that house, and if they don't buy it, you'll sell them another one.

> If you control your activities, you can influence your results.

I've often heard that agents think open houses are a waste of time. You know what? Those agents are right. Open houses are a waste of time *for them* because those agents suck at open houses. Either they don't prep appropriately for them, or they execute open houses incorrectly, with incorrect scripts or an improper mentality.

Before moving on, let me ask you this question: Where else could you be where someone who wants to buy a house will literally walk through the front door? Nowhere. And that, my fellow agents, is the benefit of holding an open house. You can put yourself in the exact spot that will draw potential clients to you.

And guess what? You *created* that opportunity to generate more business. You didn't *find* it, which means you can replicate it. And like the artists of history, you can perfect your craft and get better.

When I first started in real estate, I didn't have a massive list of people who wanted to buy or sell their homes. My wife Tara had a book of business she'd created over the years, and I suppose I could have taken her database and worked it alone. But I wanted to prove I could grow a real estate business with her as a true partner. I wanted to add value and clients to our database.

I realized early on that no one would walk up to me and say they wanted to buy a house. I've never had anyone come to my house, ring my doorbell, and ask to buy a home. Even with our office, its signage, and a corner location, only about once per quarter does someone walk into our office and say they want to buy a house.

> I realized early on that no one would walk up to me and say they wanted to buy a house.

If I was going to build my database with potential clients, holding open houses was the way to do it. When I was in multilevel marketing (not going to tell you what pyramid scheme it was), I'd go to the bookstore and take my two daughters with me. I was a young US Marine and didn't have the money to pay for babysitting, so the kids came with me. At that time, Tara worked at an Italian restaurant about twenty-five minutes from our house. We only had one car, so I dropped her off at work and went to a local big-box bookstore. I set the kids up in the children's section, walked around, and started conversations. (Don't worry; my kids were always in my sight.)

This was how I introduced myself, talked to people, and eventually invited them to know more about the product I was selling. I was a Marine from another state and didn't have a significant sphere of influence, so I went where the people were. And I found them in the bookstore.

In real estate, open houses are where the people are. Once you've worked through your sphere, you must meet new people. Open houses are the bridge between your sphere and cold calling.

Tara and I built our business with open houses. At first, I held an open house at least three out of four weekends each month. That was the only place I could be where people would walk through the door and potentially buy a house.

Myths About Open Houses

Before holding an open house, let's review the myths and misconceptions.

Myth 1: The Nosy Neighbor

You've heard that only nosy neighbors and tire-kickers come to open houses. You know who I'm talking about. A couple walks up the drive toward the house. They stop to grab a flyer and look at it briefly. You think, *Oh no, they aren't going to come in because they have the info.* But they aren't deterred. They continue toward the house. Upon entering, you exchange names and chitchat for a few moments, and they tell you they're just neighbors who came to check out the house.

Your heart sinks. *Great,* you think, *time-wasters.* The universe delivered precisely what you believed it would: time-wasters, tire-kickers, and nosy neighbors. Better yet, they stay for an hour, eat your food, and talk to you about who knows what. You're not paying attention because you think it's a lost cause.

Let me ask you some questions about these folks.

- Do they rent or own?
- If they own, how long have they lived there?
- How often does the neighborhood turn over?
- When they decide to move, what would be the reason? Downsizing? Upsizing? Closer to family?
- Never going to move? Great, they must love the area! Who do they know who might like to live there, too?
- Did you get their name, home address, and phone number?

These folks are your future listings. Create a relationship and add them to your database. Follow up with them. Become their neighborhood real estate expert. These people are your tomorrow money. You're selling a house in the future. Everyone you meet is a potential client if you do the right things.

Myth #2: Top Agents Don't Do Open Houses

Well, I do them. My wife does them. Every agent on my team does them. And many, many top agents I know do them. Why? Because it's lead generation. It's an opportunity to sell a house, increase your database, and, at the very least, get some office time. Many top agents see the value in open houses because it's one of the few places someone can buy a house from you. Top agents see value in them because they know how to prepare for them.

Myth #3: Everyone Is Already Working with an Agent.

Maybe they are, and perhaps they aren't. Who cares? Sell your listing if they're working with another agent. If I find out a potential buyer is working with an agent, I'll get both the buyers' information and their agent's—*if they know it!*

If they know their agent's contact info and they like the house, I'll call their agent, tell them the feedback, and say that I'd love to work with them on a transaction.

Let me give you some advice: Do not—I mean, do *not*—call that agent and request or demand a referral fee because the buyers walked through your open house. Don't ask for a referral fee if they bring you a contract. You were there to sell your listing, so don't jeopardize your commitment to your seller by being greedy. Sell the house. Make your clients happy.

And yet, just because they say they're working with an agent doesn't mean they aren't looking for their *next* agent. You execute on a high level, and you very well may have picked up your next client. A "Yes, I'm working with an agent" may only be a yes to say no to a salesperson. Our job is to work above the fray to win the client. If their agent isn't delivering excellent service or not working, they may lose the client. I consistently tell my team that another agent cannot steal your client; you can only give them away.

> . . . just because they say they're working with an agent doesn't mean they aren't looking for their *next* agent.

As for me, I don't ask people if they're working with an agent. It isn't in my script. Their agent's responsibility is to create a strong relationship with their client that my interactions won't interfere with. My script is a simple:

"Do you love it? Do you want to buy it?"

If the answer is yes, write the contract. If no, ask:

"What do you love? What don't you love?"

From there, I'm working to create value to sell them another home. If they're in a "committed relationship," they'll tell me.

Do the Work

You may have been to a conference or class or read a book or blog about how to prepare for an open house. Let me take you back to the theme of this book, which is to learn the fundamentals of real estate sales and perform them in a practical way—a way that you not only *can* do but also *will* do. I will give you the fundamental and simple steps for a successful open house.

To plan an open house, find out when the best time is to hold homes open in your community. I've coached agents from coast to coast, from Texas to New Jersey to Oregon, and each area has its prime time. In my market, resales are open on Sundays from 2:00 p.m. to 4:00 p.m. New construction is available from 1:00 p.m. to 5:00 p.m. Saturday is the prime time in some markets, and I know of some markets where agents hold open houses on Tuesday evenings. Do you know your market's preferred open house times? If not, ask around. Ask other agents in your office or call a few top agents and ask them.

> Let me take you back to the theme of this book, which is to learn the fundamentals of real estate sales and perform them in a practical way—a way that you not only *can* do but also *will* do.

After you set your time, the next step is to put a sign in the yard that advertises the open house. I recommend using an actual sign, not a sign rider, for your real estate sign, as it will better catch drivers' eyes.

Then what? How do you go beyond the sign? You put out directional signs—a lot of directional signs, as many directional signs as you can. A minimum, a bare minimum, should be five. If five is what it takes to weave through the neighborhood to get to the house, double that. Your goal is to drive traffic from outside the subdivision to your home. Also, you don't want to trust a potential buyer's GPS to help them find the house. It's the one time a week that most city ordinances and homeowners' associations allow you to put signs up everywhere. Check with your local board on regulations. For example, in our area, we place the *Open House, Sunday 2–4* sign in the front yard on Wednesday, but we wait until late Friday afternoon to put up all the directional signs. These directional signs are extensions of your real estate sign and brand.

Then, go beyond the sign further and market it online. Be sure to notate the open house on MLS, Zillow, Trulia, realtor.com, etc.— any online platform where the home is sold. Buyers today aren't typically just driving around on a beautiful Sunday afternoon hoping to randomly come across an open house. They are on a mission. One person drives, and the other uses their smartphone to search for what's out there. Buyers have gotten tactical in their searches, so communicate all the pertinent information in your listings.

You may be thinking, *Of course, Peter, who would* not *do these things?* You. You will not do them consistently with every open house if you don't design and implement these efforts as a standard business practice. You'll do it the first couple of times, but as time progresses, you'll forget to tell the homeowner you're holding the house open. I didn't mention that step because you would think it's obvious. But it happens. New agents ask what to do, and experienced agents forget what to do. So, make a checklist:

1. Set up a time with the homeowner to hold the home open.
2. Let the homeowner know that open houses work best if they're not there.
3. Place an open house sign with the times in the yard.
4. Put directional signs out.
5. Market open house online.

And that's it. Those are the basic steps to go beyond the sign. Now, what if you want to go bigger?

Go Big

You want more people to come to your open house? Then you will have to do some leg and phone work. To begin, call the neighbors. Some resources and websites will sell you neighborhood contact information. Call the neighbors, introduce yourself, and invite them to the open house. Be simple, be polite, and be direct.

Second, knock on some doors. *Gasp!* Calm down, I'm not asking you to go out and knock on one hundred-plus doors, just twenty. Knock on the five to the right, cross the street and knock on ten, then cross the street again and knock on five more. You've now walked a complete circle and are back at the house you're holding open. This will take about thirty to forty minutes, so plan accordingly. Don't show up twenty minutes before the open house; do it an hour before you begin. Do you want better results? Go the day before. This gives you plenty of time and the neighbors time to make plans to attend.

> To go big, you'll have to invest a little more into the open house.

To go big, you'll have to invest a little more into the open house. Buy some balloons and tie them to every directional and yard sign.

They don't need to be fancy. They're to draw attention to your signs, to get them to stand above the fray of all the other signs that line the streets. When the average person sees balloons, they think party, and who doesn't like a party?

And my personal favorite is to bake some cookies. Not because I like to eat cookies, but because when people gather in the kitchen and eat cookies, they tend to talk, allowing you the time to build rapport, find out their goals, and learn what they're looking for in a new house.

Go Bigger

Ready to step up your game? Then, it's time to invest a little more into this form of lead generation. Start by sending a mailer to the neighborhood about a week before the event. It's not your standard home flyer in the flyer box in front of the listing, but an invitation to the open house—the *event*.

Next, knock on one hundred-plus doors. That's right, one hundred-plus doors. This is a follow-up to the flyers. Your flyers introduced you and invited them to your event/open house, and now, you can use this opportunity to ask if they received your invitation. Whether they have or have not, extend them a personal invitation.

Do all these steps, and people will show up. Better yet, you'll be well on your way to being the neighborhood real estate agent of choice.

The Open House Event

Here are a few tips to help you be as successful as possible and prepared. Be sure to have these materials with you:

- MLS sheet
- Comps for the neighborhood or the area

- Neighborhood info such as schools, restaurants, parks, libraries, etc.
- Extra flyers about the home
- Sign-in sheet

You want the prospective client to leave with something of value, and you want to contribute something of value. Clients don't value a business card. They value information, and the material you give them will have your contact information. There's no need to force your card upon anyone.

When No One Is There

The goal of an open house is to have a steady flow of people coming through, but what do you do when no one is there? You may be tempted to scroll through social media, check out YouTube videos, or jump on Netflix to finish your series. Don't do that. Stay focused. It's too hard to shift gears from, *What is my friend doing on Facebook?* To, "Let me help you spend $250,000."

When Someone Is There

Remember, people don't come to open houses looking for an agent. They come to look at the home. Our goal is to win them as a client. The following are a few steps to guide you in what to do when someone shows up.

Step 1: Guide the Conversation

Notice I said to *guide* the conversation. People know when they're being sold, and they don't like it. So don't sell. Ask questions to determine their needs, not to fulfill your own.

o Get their name. Say something like this: "The owner has asked us to let them know who has dropped by and how we might get your feedback. Thanks for signing in!"
o Rely on conversation starters:
  ▪ How did you find me?
  ▪ How long have you been looking?
  ▪ Where do you live?
  ▪ Where are you looking?
  ▪ Who are you working with?
  ▪ What's your email address?
  ▪ What's a good number for you so I can ensure you received my email?
  ▪ What's your address?

You're looking for their pain. What's pushing them out of their current home and into the next? As Tony Robbins often says, "People will do more to avoid pain than to gain pleasure." (See Part 2: I Have a Lead—Now What? for a more detailed look into mindset, these questions, and other scripts to work.)

Step 2: Set the Expectation

Once you have their information, communicate the next steps.

  ▪ I will call you . . .
  ▪ Send you . . .
  ▪ Email you . . .
  ▪ Help you . . .

Now they'll know to expect your call or other communication. People would rather die than be rude. (Again, see Part 2: I Have a Lead—Now What? for a story about that.)

Step 3: Leave Them with Something of Value

Give them something to take home so they'll remember the house, the subdivision, you, your services, etc. I will repeat it: a business card isn't something of value. If you don't get their contact information but give them your card, you're a fool if you think they'll call you when they wouldn't even share their personal information. I don't give out a business card unless I have their contact information first.

Now, you have the practical steps to have a successful open house. All that's left is to leave the house as you found it and pick up all your signs. Be sure to collect all your signs. This will save you from buying more signs or leading potential clients in endless circles trying to find an open house that isn't there.

The Good

I mentioned going bigger on an open house by knocking on one hundred doors. It's a big challenge, I know. Can you knock on one hundred doors before an open house? The answer is yes, you can. You may not want to; if that's true, you likely won't. But can you knock on just twenty?

Start at the house you're holding open, go five doors down, cross the street, knock on ten doors, and knock on five doors back to your home. Use a simple script like this:

> *"Hello, I am (your name) with (your brokerage/team). I'm holding open your neighbor's home at 123 Main Street tomorrow. I just wanted to introduce myself in case you would like to come by or know someone who might be interested."*

It's that simple. Why twenty? Because twenty is better than nothing, and you can get results with just twenty.

Tara was holding a house open in one of the more prestigious subdivisions in the area. She did the five-ten-five strategy the day before the event. Just twenty houses, no more. From that, she picked up two more listings and a buyer. The number one response she received was, "Wow, thank you for introducing yourself. No agent has ever done that."

Be the agent who does what other agents aren't willing to do, and you'll succeed because you'll stand out from the thousands of other agents in your market. This wasn't early in Tara's career. At the time, we had a team of twenty agents doing over 400 transactions a year. Her mindset was—and is—that if she spends two hours holding a house open, she'll spend the extra two hours prepping for the event and making sure people show up.

> Be the agent who does what other agents aren't willing to do, and you'll succeed because you'll stand out from the thousands of other agents in your market.

Another time, we were helping an agent start his career in a city ninety minutes north of us—Tulsa, Oklahoma. He was new to the area, so he didn't have a sphere of influence or a database of people to work with. He went from zero to fourteen listings in four months—all from open houses. He found an agent in his brokerage who had listings he could hold open every Sunday for three out of four weekends a month. He then did everything to prep, including knocking on twenty doors the Saturday before he held the house open. He ensured he was on point during the event and worked the leads neighbors gave him or from the traffic to the open house. By the end of the first month, he had two listings, which grew from there.

Open houses are one of the few places where someone could walk through the door and say, "I need to buy a home."

The Bad

I'm going to tell on myself here. The habits we form, good or bad, can start from a tiny seed and grow into something big. I created a bad habit by filling my dead time at open houses with unproductive, entertaining media. What started as flipping through social media between potential clients turned into *What's on Netflix?*

This day, I got to the property early and ensured the signs were well placed and the house was prepped—all the necessary things. Then, I settled in on the couch and started to watch a movie. No one came for about an hour and fifteen minutes. So, I was pretty comfortable and deeply engrossed in my film. I was at a pivotal scene where one of the main characters was on the verge of death, his young son doing his best to save him. The enemy was nearby, a super intense scene.

And would you believe it? These people dared to walk into the house and interrupt my movie time! I paused the movie and quickly introduced myself. The quicker I could get them through the house, the faster I could return to my film. I only had about forty-five minutes left of the event and wanted to finish my movie by then. So I went to task, answered their questions, and got them on their way. Back on the couch, I picked up my iPad and thought, *What the f**k did I just do?*

I wasn't a new agent then, but I'd allowed bad habits to become terrible. You may be thinking, *I would never do that. Doesn't matter if I'm scrolling through social media or watching my series. When someone walks in, I'm going to jump right in and take care of them.*

The truth is that you can't. Let me tell you what was going on in my brain and what most likely will happen in yours. My brain was in a relaxed movie mode, and when a client came in, my brain couldn't shift out of relaxed movie mode into working real estate mode until *after* the client left. It was in the process of shifting while the clients were in the house, but it was too slow for my conscious mind to register. And it didn't entirely shift until after they'd left. I knew I'd failed at my job: to sell the house or find these potential buyers another home.

When I hold open houses, my mind is singularly focused on real estate and business. I stay off social media unless I post about the open house or a property-related post. Typically, I bring a business-related book with me, or I study market statistics. Then, when a client walks in, my mind is business focused, and I'm ready to do my best work.

Keep your mind sharp, and don't repeat my blunder.

2

FAMILY, FRIENDS, AND NEIGHBORS

F amily, friends, and neighbors—these are the folks you hope will
choose you to be their real estate agent. That might happen for
you, but it's never a guarantee. For them to choose you to be their
agent, they must think of you when they think of real estate.

You may think, *Of course, they'll think of me. I'm their friend, and they
know I'm an agent.* New agents often sell to their friends and family
because you told them about your new venture into real estate. So,
they thought of you when they needed to buy or sell. You were so
adamant and excited about your new career that they felt obligated to
work with you regardless of your lack of experience.

In a seller's market, family and friends will work with anyone, no matter their experience, because in a seller's market, a house will sell regardless of who listed it. But how do you get them to think of you when the market isn't great?

Too often, I've had an agent in my office or on a coaching call express their disappointment that their close friend had listed their house with another agent because they "didn't want to mix business with friendship and risk hurting our relationship."

That's a bullsh*t excuse—a vain attempt to maintain the friendship or family bond. Do you want to know why they didn't list with you? It's because they didn't think of you when they thought of a professional real estate agent.

Too often, we drop down into neutral and coast with this group of potential clients. Maybe you wear casual dress-down clothes when showing houses, or perhaps you're a few minutes late because they know you, and you think it's no big deal. Maybe they sense that you don't value them enough, and your lack of professionalism shows it. Or worse, you haven't even kept up with your friends, family, or neighbors about your real estate career, and you assume they'll work with you because, "Hey, they know I'm in real estate. I told them at the last family barbecue at Aunt Sally's house as I took a scoop of potato salad."

Or right after you posted your umpteenth post about an open house or a house you sold, you got upset because you saw an Instagram post from your old college roommate standing in front of their new home next to their real estate agent that isn't you. And you think, *How could my old college roommate buy a house with someone else? Didn't they see my Instagram name, "BobSellsRealEstate"?*

Throughout this book, you'll see me repeat, "Your success in real estate is directly proportional to the number of people who, when they think of real estate, think of you." (Honestly, I couldn't tell you where I first heard this, but if I was to give credit, it would be to the great Diana Kakoska.) Or to focus on that phrase for this chapter: "Your success in real estate—in terms of family, friends, and neighbors—is directly proportional to the level of professional real estate expertise they think of when they think of you."

> Throughout this book, you'll see me repeat, "Your success in real estate is directly proportional to the number of people who, when they think of real estate, think of you."

I'll never forget the first time it happened to me. I was talking to a family member excited about the house she'd just put under contract. She was having a little trouble and wanted my advice. My first thought was to poke her in the eye, followed by a quick kick to the shin. After holding back a few karate moves, I moved to my second thought: *This is my fault.*

I had to own that she didn't choose to work with me. The only way I can fix a problem is to take some ownership of it. If something is 100 percent not my fault, I take zero ownership and cannot fix it. And this was 100 percent my fault. I couldn't blame her for choosing someone else because when she thought of real estate, she thought of someone else or thought someone else would be better than me.

Now, I ensure that every family, friend, and neighbor is treated like any other client. I treat them better. You need to treat them better because these are the people you care most about in life, so why wouldn't you give them your best?

Do the Work

Step one to doing the work is to be professional—always. I love it when I go to a family or friend's house wearing a suit to conduct a listing appointment, and I get the comment, "You didn't need to dress up." Well, yes, I did. My manner of dress sets the tone that this is a business appointment, and I want them to see me at my best and give them my best.

Next, I learn about their real estate needs. This is where I notice the difference between the small talk of "How's the market?" and the serious talk of "No, really, how *is* the market?"

We have a lender friend who sends gifts to all her clients on their birthdays. It's the same gift for every client—or so I thought. On my birthday, I received the same gift as everyone else, but it was an upgraded version. So, if a regular client gets a small box of colorful macaroons, I receive a large box of colorful macaroons. I'm saying that when you give a personal gift to a family member or friend, send what you send your other clients—only better. It's a sign that you're a professional and treating your friends and family members as a professional would.

Be sure that your friends, family, and neighbors consistently remember that you're in real estate and be as professional, if not more so, as you would be with your other clients. Give them the red-carpet treatment.

The Good

Regarding the family member who didn't work with me, going forward, I was sure to keep her up to date on the real estate market and the value of her home. I kept her in our database and provided the same client touches that all our other clients received. These actions, plus the everyday interactions we had at family events, made a difference. When the time came for her to sell and purchase a new home, she called me first, not the other agent.

I didn't mention that the other agent was also her close friend. Remember that most of your family, friends, and neighbors probably know multiple agents, and there are lots to choose from. By professionally nurturing that relationship, I ensured I was the first person she thought of when she thought of real estate.

The Bad

One day, I had an agent come into my office fuming mad. A friend she'd known for years was moving to Oklahoma from another state. This agent had met them when they'd lived in Florida over ten years earlier. The two communicated almost weekly through text messages and phone calls. They were as close as friends who live in different states could be.

When her friend and family came to town on a house-hunting trip, they bought a house with another agent. Now, understand the friend knew this agent worked at the top residential real estate team in Oklahoma (which we are). It wasn't a secret. Many of their conversations had involved her day-to-day life with our brokerage and the real estate life.

When the agent confronted her friend about working with another agent she didn't know, her friend responded, "I didn't want to mix business with our friendship."

Let me ask you this question: Do you think that hurt their friendship? I can tell you that these two don't talk as often as they used to. And no, I don't think they'll be invited to the Fourth of July party.

I don't know why the friend chose to work with someone else because no one truly thinks that working with a competitor won't hurt a friendship. The reward of working with someone else must have been worth the risk of losing the friendship. To my agent's credit, she didn't toss the friendship into the hot fires of Hades. But she learned a lesson to be *intentional* from that point forward. A simple, direct conversation along the lines of, "I can't wait for you to come to town, and *I* get to show you houses. Finding your Oklahoma home is going to be so much fun. When do you plan on coming to town?" may have kept the friendship as strong as it once had been.

3

FOR SALE BY OWNER

Historically, *For Sale by Owner* (FSBO) homes comprise only about 8 percent of the residential real estate market. This percentage has decreased as technology has increased. At first, many believed that when major real estate sites opened their platforms to the public to post their properties that For Sale by Owner homes would increase; the exact opposite happened.

For Sale by Owners should be embraced and shouldn't be looked upon as competition, nor should they be feared. The owner is announcing to the world that they have a property to sell. This means two things: They're a seller and potentially a buyer. There's no need to cold call a random number and ask, "Do you plan to buy, sell, or invest in real estate in the near future?" They tell you by putting their house on the market.

Most FSBOs aren't full service, which represents an opportunity for you. Now, you can find the gap in what they're missing and fill in where they may or may not know they're deficient. Those owners/ sellers realize they have holes in marketing the sale of their home. Taking photos and posting them online with a price seems straightforward enough until they're waist-deep in all the details.

> The owner is announcing to the world that they have a property to sell. This means two things: they're a seller and potentially a buyer.

Even with technology, the complexity of selling a home has increased, and younger generations seem to recognize this. My generation and above think they can do it better on their own.

I've heard many scripts and lead generation techniques for picking up FSBOs throughout my career. Some of those were good, and some were bad. Whether a script is good or bad, real estate agents often choose one strategy to work with FSBOs, which becomes the sole strategy they live or die by. Most die by it and give up on FSBO leads after hearing many nos and the occasional yes. The nos outweighed the yeses, and the juice is not worth the squeeze when creating business elsewhere is easier. Or so agents with a singular strategy think. Don't put FSBOs in a single box.

Like any other client, you cannot have a one-size-fits-all strategy with FSBOs. When you start working with a client, you must discover their needs to create value. Once you create value for them, they are genuinely your clients. FSBOs are no different. When handled correctly, FSBO sellers will see the inherent value in your services.

When you have multiple strategies at your fingertips, you have numerous opportunities to create income for you and provide value to them. Find the plan that best suits the situation. Be ready to pivot your scripts based on your conversation. You may win the listing and sell the property. Or they might retain it as a FSBO, and you can find them their next home. You can work with FSBOs if you're flexible with your strategies. For any agent, they're a potential source of business.

Do the Work

If you're wondering where to find For Sale by Owner leads, you're not looking. Sites such as Zillow will give you all the necessary information: name, address, and phone number. There are also paid-for sites if you decide to go that route. I suggest avoiding the autodialer here, as well as the expired listings. It's not about how many people you can call in your lead generation time; it's about setting an appointment to win the listing. I say this from experience. I've done both. I've worked with a few different autodialer systems that call one to three expired FSBO/prospects at a time, and I've researched and called one prospect at a time. You may not be able to reach as many people in a short amount of time, but my experience has been that I've been more successful with the prospects I do call.

When working with FSBOs to create business, there are multiple ways to approach them, which depend on you. I say it depends on you because I've noticed that agents feel more confident and comfortable with one strategy over another. You should know all the strategies to pivot when required, but start with the one you're most comfortable with to build confidence. The five strategies are:

- Ask for the listing.
- Ask for the purchase.
- Ask for the weekend.
- Ask for the contract.
- Ask for the open house.

Ask for the Listing

Asking for the listing is just that. You call the owner to list their home when they decide to no longer try to sell it themselves. Let me give you a tip: Don't start that conversation off with a lie. There's a script often used by agents that goes something like this:

> **Liar Agent:** *"Hello, this is Bob with Sly real estate. I have a client interested in your property. Will you work with an agent on the sale of your house?"*
>
> **Honest Seller:** *"Yes, I will."*
>
> **Liar Agent:** *"Fantastic. When is a good time to come by?"*

From there, the Liar Agent shows up at the property without a client and uses some variation of why their client couldn't make it and says, "I'm here to walk through for them." From that point, they spill out a presentation to win the listing.

I'm not going to say this strategy doesn't work. But I don't think you should ever start a relationship with a lie. And you have to ask yourself, if you're willing to lie for the business in the small stuff, will you eventually lie for the big stuff, which could get you sued or cause you to lose your license? Be a straight shooter and be direct.

Here's a simple script:

> **Agent:** *"Hello, this is (name) with (brokerage). I'm working with multiple buyers who might be interested in your property. Is there a time I could do a quick walk-through to see if it fits any of my buyers' needs?"*
>
> **Seller:** *"I don't think that would be a problem. When would you like to come by?"*
>
> **Agent:** *"Does today at 3:00 p.m. work for you?"*

When you're at the property, you can see if it fits your buyers' needs. If so, set up a time to bring them back. If not, give the seller feedback about why it's not a fit.

Here's a script you can use when talking to the owner on the phone:

Agent: *"How long have you been on the market?"*

Seller: *"About ___ weeks"*

Agent: *"Wow, _____ weeks!"* *(Note: Always make it a big deal even if it's only been a week.)*

Agent: *"In _____ weeks, how many offers have you received?"*

Seller: *_____*

Agent: *"Wow, in_____ weeks!"* *(Note: Always sound shocked. If they've received one or more offers, then proceed with:*

Agent: *"So you received _____ offers, but none that could be negotiated to terms you would accept?"* *(Note: Pause for dramatic effect or a response, then continue…*

Agent: *"At some point, if your house doesn't sell, you'll have to change your price or marketing plan. Have you thought about which one you plan to change?"*

From here, you'll often find that sellers will want to talk about what you think the price should be or how to change the marketing. That's when I start going for the listing and say: "Do you mind if I walk through your house again? When I came through the first time, I had *my buyers* in mind as their agent. Let me walk through again with the eyes of a listing agent *for you.*"

Ask for the Listing

Agent: *"Hello, this is (name) with (brokerage). We've never met before, and I wanted to take the opportunity to introduce myself. I'm working with multiple buyers who may be interested in your property. Would you be willing to work with an agent on the sale if I brought a buyer to you?"*

Seller: *"Yes, if you brought a buyer, I would pay _____%."*

Agent: *"When agents list properties, sellers agree to list for a certain period of time before they can interview other agents. Have you set a time for how long you'll market the property before interviewing someone to step in if it doesn't sell?"*

Seller: *"No, I haven't thought much about that."*

Agent: *"I understand. I only ask because this is our first time speaking. If you decide to list it, I'd like the opportunity. Is there a convenient time to stop by, introduce myself in person, and possibly walk through the house to see if it fits any of my buyers' needs or wants?"*

Seller: *"Um, not sure."*

Agent: *"Just let me know a time that works best for you. I don't want to put you out. Would Sunday at 1:00 p.m. work for you? I'm holding another house open at 2:00 p.m. so I could come by right before then."*

Note: The idea behind this script is to use words such as *convenient* and *best,* and by suggesting a specific time, you make it easy for them to say yes. Also, saying you have a 2:00 p.m. appointment shows two things: You won't linger, and you're doing your job by holding an open house. Finally, when you're at the property, you could launch into the *Ask for the Weekend* or *Ask for the Open* with:

Agent: *"I haven't scheduled an open house for next Sunday yet. Would you be open to me holding your home open next Sunday from 2:00 p.m. to 4:00 p.m.?"*

If yes…

Agent: *"Great, I can do it two ways—by putting out signs that show it's open (Ask for the Open), or I can maximize it by marketing it just for the weekend (Ask for the Week). Which do you prefer?"*

Ask for the Purchase

> *Agent:* *"Hello, this is (name) with (brokerage). First, I'm not calling to try to list your house. I'm calling to ask where you'll be moving when your house sells."*

> *If local or not:* *"Are you currently working with an agent to help you find your next home?"*

In this script, you can work to pick them up as a buyer or refer them to someone in another area to earn a referral fee. Find the buyer's needs (discussed in Chapter 13) and keep going. With just two simple questions, you could have a sale. Here are a few more variations of this script:

Ask for the Weekend

> *Agent:* *"Hello, this is (name) with (brokerage). I saw your property is for sale, and you're selling it yourself. I'm calling to see if you'd be open to me listing your home just for the weekend?"*

Note: Wait for a response. If the answer is no, then move to the FSBO as buyer script:

> *Seller:* *"Um, what does that mean?"*

> *Agent:* *"What I'd like to do is take pictures on Thursday, list the house on Friday to include my full marketing plan, hold the house open on Sunday, and the listing expires on Monday if I don't sell it. Oh, and you get to keep the photos if it doesn't sell."*

Note: Let the seller know that for you to list and market the property for any time, you have to have a written contract. Regarding commission, you decide. Commissions are negotiable.

Ask for the Contract

Agent: *"Hello, this is (name) with (brokerage). I saw that your property is for sale, and you're selling it yourself. Congratulations on that. First, let me say that I'm not calling to try and list your house. I'm calling because I offer my services to sellers when they've found a buyer for their property. I assist them with the contract and coordinate all the parties involved, such as lenders, titles, attorneys, etc. Have you already found a professional to help you with that portion of selling your house?"*

Seller: *"Well, no. I've sold a house before and never needed anyone else."*

Agent: *"I understand. Many sellers have said the same thing. But as the market has changed over the years, they would like someone else to handle all the details and facilitate the contract as a third party to ensure everything moves smoothly. It helps sellers negotiate better when they say a third party will handle the contract."*

Seller: *"How much do you charge for that service?"*

Agent: *"I can do all that for just _____, payable at the closing of the property. If it doesn't close, you pay nothing."*

Note: You can send them disclosures if they don't already have them. Second, now you're in a position to contact the seller regularly and be their agent when they decide to hire one. As long as you let them know you can also do that. Don't assume they know, or you'll get a rude awakening when they tell you they listed with someone else and no longer need your services. When the seller agrees to pay a fee for the contract, it's an easy mental leap for them to move to a full listing because it's "just a bit more." Again, it's where emotion and logic meet.

Ask for the Open House

This is the easiest of the scripts where you ask the seller to hold their house open.

Agent: *"Hello, this is (name) with (brokerage). I noticed you have your home for sale. I'm not calling to try and list your house. I'm calling to see if you would allow me to hold your house open this Sunday to find you a buyer—or at least get you some honest feedback."*

Seller: *"What does that mean?" (Or a variation of this)*

Agent: *"Just like no one says, 'Wow, that's an ugly baby,' people often don't give honest feedback to owners, which keeps many For Sale by Owner from overcoming objections or knowing what to improve to sell their house. If you let me hold it open, I can, at the very least, get you honest feedback to assist you if I don't find a buyer for you."*

Seller: *"If you find a buyer, how much do I pay you?"*

Agent: *"We would negotiate a 3 percent of the sales price commission for bringing a buyer, so not the full listing commission. So, you'll still save money on the transaction."*

From here, it's just working out the details. Be sure to check your state's marketing rules/laws around posting an open house for a property you don't have a Listing Agreement for.

Text Messages to reach out to FSBOs

This is a bottom rung of the ladder tactic because it's highly passive. This approach will more than likely get you more nos than yeses. You can create a keyboard shortcut on your phone if your CRM doesn't support text messaging. Example text scripts are:

Text: *"Hello, this is (name) with (brokerage). I saw your home is for sale. When it sells, will you be staying local?"*

Text: *"Hello, this is (name) with (brokerage). Are you willing to work with a real estate agent if I brought you a buyer?"*

Response Scripts

The following are scripted lines that you can learn. These one-off scripts can be pulled from memory when a conversation dictates. Remember, you aren't learning scripts to play a part in a movie. You're learning scripts so that when a conversation detours, you aren't at a loss for words. You may start a conversation with one script and jump to another as the conversation continues. Be flexible and knowledgeable; never be at a loss for words.

> *Agent:* *"Statistically, the national average says 9 percent of For Sale by Owners sell their home themselves and that 91 percent eventually align themselves with a real estate professional."*

> *Agent:* *"As you can see, I'm bold in my approach to my real estate career. If you decide you want to work with an agent, I hope you'll keep me in mind as someone who works to get properties sold and doesn't wait for someone else to do my job for me."*

The Good

The easiest FSBO I ever won was as easy as picking up a flyer in front of a house. I'd just dropped off my clients after showing properties. Unfortunately, we hadn't found one they liked. I pulled out of the neighborhood and took a different route than I had when driving in, and I came across a For Sale by Owner sign with a flyer box.

I pulled to the curb, stepped out of my vehicle, and got a flyer. As I looked at it, a man came out of the house and asked, "Are you interested in seeing inside?"

I was honest with him from the beginning and used a takeaway approach. "No, thank you. I'm a real estate agent and wanted to see if your house met my current clients' criteria. Unfortunately, it doesn't," which was the truth.

"Well, that's a first," he said.

"What's that?" I asked.

"Do you know how many agents have called and told me they had a buyer for our house, and when they got here, they didn't? But they'd be happy to list it for us."

"Well, that sucks. I apologize for that. I don't think you should start any relationship with a lie. Oh, and my name is Peter Levinson." I introduced myself and held out my hand.

"Hi, I'm Bill Smith." He looked at me, how I dressed, and at my car. "Seems like you're pretty successful."

I smiled. "Thank you."

"I think I want to list my house with you if you want."

Yes, that was the easiest FSBO property I ever listed. Honestly, I never had another one that easy, but some have been close. I've learned that for every problematic client, there's an easy one, too.

The Bad

It was early in my real estate career, but I'll never forget how noticeably frustrated the title company closer seemed during the closing process. She was doing a great job, but she seemed distracted and flustered. Our deal went pretty smoothly, and the buyer and seller were happy. So, I knew it had nothing to do with our transaction.

When the client portion of the transaction was complete, the congratulations and handshakes were done, and my clients left for their new home, I went back to the closing room to wait for my file.

The closer came into the office and handed me a legal-sized folder with office documents and checks. Instead of thanking her and leaving as usual, I asked, "Everything okay? I noticed you didn't seem like yourself today."

With a deep sigh, she sat back in her chair, looked me in the eyes, and said, "You would not believe what we're dealing with right now."

Oh, this didn't sound good. What would frazzle her so much? So, I sat back in my chair as my curiosity grew.

"We closed a transaction last week where the seller was a For Sale By Owner. He accepted over fifty contracts on his home with at least $1,000 in earnest money for each one he (air quote) held. He closed on one of those contracts with us and kept everyone else's earnest money. So, now we have many angry buyers coming out of the woodwork, calling us, and wanting to know why someone else moved into the home they have under contract. They want to know where their money is."

That's the short version of the story, but you get the gist of what transpired. I don't tell you this story to paint FSBOs in a negative light or as Ponzi scheming reprobates. But in the real estate world, they may not be as regulated as we are, so be sure to dot your i's and cross your t's.

4

EXPIRED LISTINGS

A real estate market is determined by the months of available inventory. Months inventory means that if no other properties came on the market, it would take X months to sell through the currently available homes. This chapter is written for a real estate market with three-plus months of inventory. It applies even more so in a buyer's market, around six-plus months of inventory. But even when the average days on the market are less than ten, you can still find expired listings in a seller's market.

In a neutral-to-buyer's market, expired listings abound. They're like mistreated alley cats. To some, they look too far gone to mess with—why risk getting clawed up? But these alley cats, with a little of the correct type of love, can create business opportunities for you.

The benefit of cold-calling expired listings is that they've already been on the market. They represent sellers who decided to sell when it wasn't the most optimal time. They are cold calls only because these sellers don't know you yet. They're probably lukewarm; you must discover their original motivation to sell, reconnect them to that goal, and turn them into new clients.

> The benefit of cold-calling expired listings is that they've already been on the market. They represent sellers who decided to sell when it wasn't the most optimal time.

Understanding the homeowner's mindset who has an expired listing is essential. FSBO owners and expired listings owners are on opposite ends of the spectrum. FSBOs believe the best about their house and think they're the best to sell it. Their mindset is, "It's going to sell, and I can do it myself." On the other hand, those who have expired listings may have started out optimistic. An agent made grand promises to sell their home in record time. But their house didn't sell, and their dreams of flowing equity have been smashed.

Their beloved home was rejected. Days passed with that glaring real estate sign staring back at them whenever they looked out their front window or left the house. They had little to no showings. They felt they had done their part by prepping their home to be shown. They cleaned the house like never before. They decluttered and stowed away personal items. As a family, they'd planned what they would do after the home sold. Instead, they were disappointed as the days and months went by. Their dreams and goals got farther and farther away.

Mostly, they were disappointed in their listing agent. Indeed, it had to be her fault. Their house was better than all the others that had sold or were on the market. What had their agent been doing all these months?

Some expired listings may have had multiple showings. For six months, they'd endured showing after showing of their property. They'd had to leave at a moment's notice to accommodate a showing in hopes of receiving an offer. If or when they received an offer, it was low. These sellers also lay the blame on the agent. *My agent must not be selling my home right,* they think. *How could the offers be so low? Didn't they tell the other agent how much I spent to upgrade from 2 cm to 3 cm granite?*

Now that they've been burned, they want to slow down, hoping they'll find the right agent this time. They get bombarded with phone calls by hopeful agents. This isn't unusual. On average, an expired seller has been contacted eight to ten times by the time we speak to them—and that doesn't include the mailbox full of letters from agents who say they would have sold the home if given the chance.

As time has passed, the seller's goals may have changed. They still want to sell, but not for the same reasons. Understanding why they're selling and discovering their motivation is essential. More than likely, the last agent promised to sell their home, and when the listing expired, they made more promises to keep the listing. Their new approach? Lower the price well below the original estimated net to the seller.

Then there's the overpriced listing that never reduced the price, no matter how often the agent shared comparable properties or feedback. These sellers start working with a new agent at the price you'd been trying to get them to all those months. Of course, it sells at the correct market price within a few weeks. Their new agent is the hero.

This could be you. Just as it happens *to* you, it can happen *for* you. Another agent has done the work, and you get to walk in and list the home at a price the other agent originally suggested. That's how it works—but it only works if you make the calls.

What's Stopping You?

What do you have to lose? No, really, *what do you have to lose?* That's what I realized before I made my first cold call. There was nothing an expired listing could take from me; I could only gain by calling. The biggest obstacle to cold calling or following up with leads is the fear of rejection. Seriously, ask yourself why you won't make the call. Agents get into real estate because they want to help someone. Well, someone needs to sell their house, and you won't call to help them?

Are you afraid of rejection? No, you're scared of *someone else* rejecting you. If you fail to make calls when you know you should, you've already rejected yourself. You've become someone who thinks so little of yourself that you're afraid another person will say no. I'll make you a deal. Here's my phone number: 405-532-6969. Every time you call someone and feel rejected, call me next. I'll tell you how f**king awesome you are. Because you're doing something others are too afraid to do.

When a telemarketer calls me, I say, "Hey buddy, great job. I won't buy from you, but I love that you called. I will let you go so you can get on to the next call. Good luck, you got this." And I hang up. I want to stay strong against being afraid to call people. Because if I get annoyed, frustrated, or angry when a solicitor calls me, that will get ingrained in my subconscious mind. I'll assume that when I call a prospective listing, they'll feel annoyed, frustrated, and angry. Instead, I reinforce that I'm proud of people who make cold calls because I think sellers are pleased when I call them. Change how you think, and how you think about the world will change.

> Change how you think, and how you think about the world will change.

I now have no fear of cold calling out of the blue. That can be you. All you must do is get comfortable with the scripts (we'll get to those in a minute), be comfortable in who you are, and be comfortable being uncomfortable making calls—until you become comfortable making calls.

Do the Work

I differ from many real estate coaches and trainers here. I don't recommend being on a dialer and burning through expired seller leads as quickly as your dialer will let you. Yes, it's a numbers game, but how about you play smarter than the rest?

Prep

Before calling an expired seller, take a moment to familiarize yourself with the property. Look at the photos, the marketing, who had it listed, etc. Ask yourself:

1. What did the agent do well?
2. What would you do differently?
3. What will you improve on?
4. Why do you think it didn't sell?

When you call, the seller may ask questions about the property like those above. This isn't the time to dazzle them with your bullsh*t; it's time to impress them with what you know about the property. Don't give away everything you know initially; that would give away all your value. A simple response to add to your scripts is:

"I've done some analysis on your house, and I'd like to walk through it to validate my findings. Is today at 3:00 p.m. a good time for you?"

When calling expired listings, you need to be script-ready, know how to overcome objections, and be savvy enough not to be a jerk. The seller isn't going to be neutral about your call. They'll either be defensive or be on the offense. The first objective of the script is to allow them to feel in control. Their defensive or offensive attitude is an attempt to stay in control. Their house hasn't sold, and now many real estate agents are calling to say how they could have done a better job. So, concede control to the seller. Let them say no to you in response to a few controlled questions, such as:

"Have you decided you no longer want to sell your house?"

"Do you think your agent marketed the house to its fullest potential?"

"Have your goals changed since you first listed your home?"

This last one is my favorite because it lets them open up and talk about themselves. When I teach scripting in my office, I tell the agents, "You can win the appointment and not get the listing." You can use a script full of all the yes responses, then show up at the property and no one's home. Or even worse, you could go through the whole appointment and not list the house.

Agents who power their way through with sellers are script bullies. They have all the answers and objections to get the yeses they want to hear, but the seller never intends to sign the listing paperwork. The seller may say yes, but their yes is a no. After all, the easiest way to tell a salesperson no is to tell them yes and then not follow through.

When you first attempted to ride a bike, you probably fell. And the second time, and the third—it's part of the learning process. So, don't be afraid to fail. Embrace it. Just fall forward. Stick to the scripts. Don't change the script if it doesn't work the first time, second time, third time, etc. Stick to the script. Look for patterns in the objections you receive and practice scripts for those.

When you call expired listing owners, you won't have a 100 percent success rate. But with practice and repetition, your success rate will improve. Call by call. Day by day. If and when you modify the script, it will be when you feel ready to insert your personality into it, not out of fear of rejection.

Remember that expired sellers don't know you as your sphere or previous clients do. Could you find a connection between you and this expired listing prospect? Take time to do a little research. Calling expired listings is a numbers game,

> When you call expired listing owners, you won't have a 100 percent success rate. But with practice and repetition, your success rate will improve.

and you can increase your odds of success with a bit of research. Social media is the go-to. Do you have friends in common on Facebook? Do you have the same followers or follow the same people on Instagram? Do you have any connections on LinkedIn? If so, you can call and request a reference. Here's what I've done:

> *"Hey Bob, this is Peter Levinson. I was calling to see if you could do me a favor. We have a friend in common (Seller). I am contacting (Seller) to help them sell their home. Would you mind if I mentioned you as a reference?"*

Notice the script does not say *use* you as a reference. Words are powerful, and our subconscious mind is always listening. You don't want the reference to feel they are being *used*.

Where to Find Numbers for Expired Listings

Many services in the marketplace will sell the data. Your CRM may already provide it. I'm not here to endorse any site. Plus, something new may be available by the time this book prints or a year after publication. Technology changes, but scripts are tried and true. But I will give this advice: Don't be limited by the most recent expired listings. Depending on the cycle your real estate market is currently in (buyer or seller market), you may be able to research properties that expired much earlier. For example, we called sellers during the down curve when the market started recovering. Some hadn't been listed for over two years. All we had to do was modify the questions a little:

"Your house was listed about a year ago. Did your plans change, and you no longer need to sell?"

"If I sold your house, would you still (repeat what they told you)?"

"When it was listed, about _____ homes sold. I mention that because I was wondering if you felt everything had been done to get your house sold for you?"

"What do you think could have been done differently?"

"What were your goals in selling your house?"

"Have those goals changed?"

"What if I sold your house? Would that help you achieve your goals?"

In this section, the scripts are presented in a start-to-finish manner. You need to practice, write out, and memorize them. Every call will start with *"Hello, this is (your name) with (brokerage)."* From there, you can launch into any of the questions above. The script you use will depend on what you find out about the property or the seller.

When I ask a seller why they think their house didn't sell, I often get this answer:

Seller: *"I don't know why. My agent never gave me feedback."*

Agent: *"Interesting. Would you be open to me walking through your house to give you feedback? From what I see in my analysis of your property, I have an idea, but I'd like to validate my findings before I give you my opinion about why that agent couldn't get it sold."*

Here's another question to ask:

Agent: *"Do you feel your house was priced right compared to similar homes?"*

Seller: *(Yes, no, what do you think?)*

Agent: *"From what I see in my analysis of your property, you may be 100 percent correct. But I'd like to validate my findings before I give you my final opinion about the market value of your property."*

Notice this script always leads back to a walk-through of the property—an appointment. The goal is to get an appointment. If the seller says they already have an agent:

Agent: *"So you have already signed the listing paperwork?"*

Seller: *"No, not yet."*

Agent: *"Then you still have time to interview me before you're locked into a listing agreement with another agent. I am available today at _____. Does that work for you?"*

Now, make some calls!

The Good

An agent on my team became a hero of mine for going above and beyond for a client. Ron had been working with a buyer for some time, and they'd missed out on a property they'd made an offer on. The property had gone into multiple offers, and they lost despite coming in way over the asking price. This frustrated the buyers. They began to wonder if they should wait to find their next home.

Ron kept up with them and continued showing them similar houses, but the buyers rejected them. Ron felt they were stuck on the house they had missed out on. So Ron asked a great question: "What was it about that house that you loved so much?"

"It wasn't the house we loved," they said. "It was the neighborhood. We love that subdivision. We wanted to live here a few years back but missed an opportunity."

Ron had a problem to solve. The real estate market inventory was at an all-time low. The average days on the market were less than fifteen days. Decent homes sold in days with multiple offers well above the listed price. There were no homes available in that neighborhood.

Ron asked, "How did you miss the opportunity to move into the subdivision?"

"There was a house we liked, but the seller took it off the market before we put an offer on it."

"Do you remember where this property was?" Ron asked.

"We don't remember. We know it was in this neighborhood."

"Let's see if we can find that home," Ron responded

Ron asked his buyers to drive through the neighborhood until they found the property. When he knew the address, Ron did some research. The property had been listed two years prior but expired on the market, and the sellers didn't list it again.

Ron didn't have the sellers' contact information, so he did the next best thing. He knocked on the door and used the following script:

Agent: *"Hello, I am Ron Thompson with the Levinson Real Estate Team. I have a real buyer interested in your house and ready to make an offer. If I brought you an offer, would you be willing to look at it?"*

Seller: *"I'm not sure."*

Agent: *"Your house was on the market a few years ago and didn't sell. Was there a reason you decided not to put it back on the market?"*

Seller: *"We felt the timing wasn't right since it didn't sell."*

Agent: *"With an offer in hand, do you feel the timing would be right now?"*

Seller: *"I'm not sure. I'd have to talk to my spouse."*

Agent: *"Of course. When will he be home?"*

Seller: *"Around 6:00 p.m."*

Agent: *"Great. I'll come back at 6:30."*

When Ron returned, he had an offer from his buyers slightly above market value but not nearly as much as the house that had gone to multiple offers. Because it was off-market, there weren't any other buyers to drive up the price, and the sellers felt they were getting a great deal—especially since it was more than what they'd previously listed two years earlier.

Let's look at the scripting Ron used. In Ron's introduction, he introduced himself and said, "I have a *real* buyer." Second, he kept listening for objections and overcoming them before they got too big. For example, the second objection was having to talk to the spouse. Ron found out when the spouse would be home and set the appointment himself. He didn't ask if he could come back. He said he'd be back at 6:30 to talk to them both.

Ron succeeded in selling his buyers that house and earning a 3 percent commission by finding an expired listing from years earlier. History is full of expired listings. Go find some!

The Bad

The builder had just finished giving me a tour of the vacant home. The builder had asked us to look at his homes and tell him why they hadn't sold. This property and a few others in the addition had been listed for a while and failed to sell.

"From what I can tell," I said. "Your last agent was terrible. The marketing photos were just plain bad." I then unleashed an avalanche of criticism of the previous agent's ineptitude to properly market and sell these homes. At the end of my twenty-minute onslaught, the builder said, "Mom has always been able to sell my homes in the past."

I caught my breath. Did he just say *Mom?*

He looked at me, and I looked at him. I broke the silence with, "Well, now I feel like an asshole." I don't usually use that type of language with a client, but it was time to fall on the sword.

Thankfully, he laughed. And yes, I did list the properties. But more importantly, I learned a valuable lesson. Never disparage the previous agent. You don't know the seller's relationship with them, and you might insult someone's mom to their face.

5

MARKET YOURSELF

This chapter introduces the basic marketing principles to help you develop your brand. In real estate, you continuously market your properties and yourself. I'll guide you to build your brand to market yourself.

Let's look at commercial agents, since it's a little easier for them to brand themselves than residential agents. The commercial real estate industry is already broken down into small sections like industrial, hotels, restaurants, commercial offices, etc. A commercial agent who wants to specialize in a particular field must choose and work in that field.

Residential real estate is different. It's filled with various price points, areas, types of residential properties, etc. If you're going for a niche market, then you have a defined path to follow. Luxury real estate agents will focus on all things luxury. A mid-town/downtown agent will focus on all things in that area. Same for historic property agents. If you're like most agents and don't want to or can't confine yourself to a specific niche, then you must build a personal brand that appeals to the masses.

You are you. Your business isn't you. Your real estate business is what you do. Clients and potential clients will check social media to see who you are as a person and decide if you're the type of person they want to know and do business with. However, marketing yourself goes beyond social media.

Social media is one small aspect of how you market yourself. It's what someone may see before they meet the real you. If LinkedIn is a social media business resume, consider the other social sites as an overview of who you are. On social media platforms, you must simultaneously think of yourself as a celebrity and a potential political candidate. So, what does the real you look like?

What you put online needs to match what people meet in person, or they'll feel deceived. Here's an example. It was early in my career, and I'd decided to wear a suit to the office that day. As I was working at my desk, which was directly in line with the doorway to our office, agents could walk by and easily see me. One agent walked by and, in passing, he looked at me and said, "Nice suit. Have a closing today?"

Even though it sounded like a question, I knew it wasn't. It was a statement that made me think, *Is that how I'm perceived? Is the perception that I only dress up when I have a closing? What have I looked like all the other days?*

For the most part, real estate agents don't have a dress code. We can wear what we want when we want. I've toured luxury properties with buyers where the listing agent showed up in a yoga pants and a T-shirt. She may have just come from a yoga class; however, my clients didn't care about her yoga schedule. As we were leaving, the wife said, "How unprofessional." Even though she wasn't their agent, they felt disrespected. I should also note that the wife who said that owns a fitness studio—a fitness studio! It was another ah-ha moment in personal branding.

A retail business typically has a dress code for its store, which presents a particular image to the public. Before joining Tara in real estate, I ran retail stores. I made it mandatory to wear polishable dress shoes, no wrinkled pants, and a store shirt. It was simple, but I wanted to present a professional staff to the public. Not the image of, "Hey Buddy, I'm only here 'til 5:00 p.m. because I have to be. So, hurry up and buy something so I can go on break."

In my real estate business, I needed to decide what image I wanted the public and my clients to see. Was it the fun, hip agent? The agent in a suit and tie? The casual, golf-polo agent? The suit and T-shirt agent? The agent who always wore a branded logo shirt? The T-shirt-and-jeans, easygoing agent? Whatever you want your image to be, you must decide and be consistent.

I decided to dress in a suit every day. My goal is to always be a business professional. It wasn't long before clients would comment, "You must be the sharpest dressed man in real estate." I've even had clients and other agents call to ask me where to get a suit because they had an important event coming up. Whenever a client thinks of me, it's a win.

What I wore was just one aspect of my branding. I began to do other things to build my brand. I wanted to be known as a leader and teacher in the industry, so I posted videos of book reviews, motivational talks, and teaching on leadership and motivational topics, etc. This is what I'm passionate about. So, I used my passion to create my brand.

Do the Work

Now it's your turn. Get a notebook and answer these questions to build your brand:

- **Who are you?** Seems like a simple enough question, but it's one of the hardest for people to answer. Before you decide on your brand, figure out who you are. Know who you are, and you know who you market to.
- **What's your resume?** Are you a college alumnus? Are you a veteran? What's your previous experience? Build your resume as if you're going to hand it to a client. Because you will.
- **What are your hobbies?** Your hobbies can be incorporated into your branding, from the movies you watch to the sports you play.
- **What are you passionate about (other than real estate)?** This goes along with your hobbies. What can you use to talk about real estate without talking about real estate?
- **What do you want the public to know about you?** This is important. You may not want everything to be part of your public figure. And that's fine. Decide now, and build your brand. Jim Carrey said it best: "Jim Carrey is a character I play."
- **How do you want clients to perceive you?** I like to go to the gym and lift weights, but I rarely post pictures and photos of my gym time. When I do, I use it to show that I'm pushing myself to reach my personal best. I know other agents who regularly post their workouts and charity runs they participate in. They've built a community around their hobby.

You may be thinking, *I want to be authentic with my clients*. I agree, but not everything in your life must always be shared. Maybe you'll create two different social media accounts. One can be for the public and include what you want them to see about you, the real estate agent. The other can be a private account for all your polarizing views or the wild life you lead. That may be harsh, but unless you plan on getting into politics or only working with clients who align with you politically, you may want to consider this. Have you stopped or thought about not using a product because someone who endorsed it or a leader of that company said something you disagreed with for a political or religious reason? Do you want your clients to do the same thing?

For the first ten years of my real estate career, I never posted photos of myself when I traveled, even though I traveled a lot. I didn't want to create the perception that I wasn't working when I was out of town. I wanted my clients to think I was always on the job. And when a client discovered that I worked an entire transaction while I was in Italy or negotiated a contract snowboarding down a mountain, they would say things like, "Man, you work hard. You should have enjoyed your vacation." But if they'd known I was gone, they'd be frustrated because they were making one of the most significant purchases of their life, and I was on a beach in Mexico. On the other end of the spectrum, I know agents who travel often, post and share everything, and have successful careers. Their brand is different from mine, but it works for them. Figure out what works for you.

Get Reviews

Like a restaurant, you'll need to build up your reviews. When the public wants to know about you, they can read what others have said. Currently, the five top sites are:

1. Google
2. Facebook

3. Zillow
4. realtor.com
5. Yelp

If you want to build your reviews, you'll need to ask your clients for them—which means you need to do a five-star job if you want a five-star review. Whenever you receive a review, respond and thank the client. It's always polite to thank someone for a compliment, and when you receive a negative review, you'll look less defensive when you respond.

> If you want to build your reviews, you'll need to ask your clients for them—which means you need to do a five-star job if you want a five-star review.

What about negative reviews? I'm going to give Grant Cardone credit here. I once heard him say, "There's no such thing as a bad review."

At first, I thought, *Yes, there is Grant. Look what this asshole said about me.*

You know you thought the same thing when someone trash-talked you or your business. But, following his advice, I stopped trying to get every negative review removed, and I found a way to respond in a way that made myself, my agent, or my company look good (or as good as possible). Here's an example from an actual Google review:

Review: If I could give lower than one star, I would. We moved from Colorado to Edmond, and unfortunately, we had to work with Tara and her team. They are absolutely unprofessional in every sense of the word. They always waited until the last second for deadlines and extended one deadline in particular up until three days before we were supposed to move in. The deal almost didn't go through. Tara doesn't care about every buyer. She has her little minions that do the work for her, and there's a lack of communication between them. Finally, the listing agent didn't even drop off our keys or garage door opener at the title company. The way they try to defend themselves in these 1-star reviews just goes to show you how out of touch they are. Why try to defend yourself? Why don't you just apologize and admit your shortcomings?

Our Response: *As you were not a client of ours, your experience with our team was through your agent. It's unfortunate she injected so much emotion into the transaction. We find it more beneficial to all parties involved if we don't place blame on others when working through the intricacies of a complex transaction just to make ourselves appear better to our clients. Such as in this transaction, our client had a great experience and was appreciative of how we handled items such as pressuring the insurance company to come out two weeks earlier than scheduled. As well as kept the transaction together. If you would like more specifics, please feel free to reach out to me directly. You may find knowing both sides to be enlightening. (405) 532-6969.*

You are correct in your updated response. I apologize for the poor service from your agent. While she wasn't an agent affiliated with our company, I do my best to work within the real estate community to promote training, education, and professionalism. Unfortunately, I can only directly influence the agents who work for me.

You'll see this one and others if you search our Google reviews. But you know what? I've lost count of the clients who said they read our reviews and decided to work with us because of the negative ones. If you have 300 five-star reviews and not one negative one, people don't feel like they're seeing the true you. They think you've paid for the reviews. And if you have enough transactions, someone will get mad. We've sold over 500 homes per year for years. We've completed thousands of transactions and worked with thousands of people. We will not make everyone happy, and neither will you. So, get some reviews and respond to them accordingly.

Here's a simple script to solicit reviews:

"Hello, I really enjoyed working with you. If you gave me a review, would it be five stars?"

If yes, *"Fantastic, if I sent you a link, would you be so kind as to put that in writing on (site)? It would be appreciated."*

If no, *"Thank you so much for sharing. It's feedback like this that helps me get better. I appreciate your honesty and will make it a priority to improve in this area."*

Of course, don't send someone the review link if they said they wouldn't give you a five-star review.

Tell Your Story

This was one of the hardest things for Tara and me to do. Our real estate coach would always say we were "undercover agents." We focused on the clients, marketed our properties, and prospected for leads. Telling our story was at the bottom of the list of things we wanted to do. But without telling our story, others created an account for us. Competitors made up stories about who we were and what we did.

Agents would say at appointments, "Tara is so busy that you'll never get hold of her." Every call we got, no matter how big, went to her cell phone. She's carried two phones for more years than I can remember.

> ... we had to start creating content that told our story so others wouldn't make something up. You need to shape your narrative.

One of the funniest was when owners/brokers of other companies would tell agents that "it's mandatory to work out to be on our team" to persuade agents away from our team or brokerage. We promote physical health first. After all, how do you expect to perform at a high level if your body is subpar? If you lack physical discipline, mental discipline is that much harder. So, we had to start creating content that told our story so others wouldn't make something up. You need to shape your narrative.

Video

You've already answered a few questions that define what you want to be known for. So, get a camera and start recording your story. There are a couple of strategies for creating videos. One is to create individual content for each platform, and the other is to build long videos and edit them for platforms as you see fit.

For example, you could shoot a ten-to-thirty-minute video on a specific topic. You can edit the video and upload highlights to various platforms. The full video could go on YouTube, three- to five-minute splices could go on Facebook, and you could post one-minute cuts to TikTok or Instagram Reels. Each smaller video could point viewers to the full-length video on your YouTube channel.

Or you could create content specific for each platform. Facebook is the social party, Instagram the look-at-me photos/videos, TikTok quick entertainment, etc. Play to the strengths of that social media platform and the image you want to portray. The main thing to do is start shaping or reshaping your business persona.

The Good

I have an agent on my team who uses the "Realtor (HisName)" Instagram handle. I know what you're thinking—that's pretty normal. What makes this a good story? What if I told you that he rarely posts about real estate on his Instagram page? Instead, he's an avid cyclist and belongs to several riding groups, so he posts pics of his bike, him on his bike, snapshots of maps from his rides, and so on. In his cycling group, he's known as the Realtor.

He once invited me to ride a seventeen-mile trail south of the Oklahoma City metro area. The trail looped back and forth, frequently coming close to where we'd just been or would be. In his bright blue "kit" (the skin-tight shirt and shorts he insists on wearing), he stood out in the treeless fall woods. From the trailhead, through the woods, to loading our bike, I lost count of the times I heard, "It's Realtor," "Hey Realtor," or other ways to say hello to Realtor.

Most agents create the "Realtor Name" or change their name to "Realtor Name" and post open houses, for sale properties, real estate tips, etc., repeatedly. And they wonder why they don't receive any interaction. His name is just that, Realtor "Name". Everything else in his Instagram posts is what he likes to do and ways to interact with people on the platform. And when someone in his circle has a real estate need, they think of him. Again, your success in real estate is directly proportional to the number of people who, when they think of real estate, think of you.

The Bad

I received a text message from a lender partner: *You will never believe what this agent put on my friend's door today.* The friend in question lived in a desirable historic part of town where homes are at the upper end of the price range for the Oklahoma City market.

The three dots that bounced in the bubble let me know more was coming via text. A photo finally appeared on my phone. It depicted a door hanger. On the door hanger was a shirtless man lying in bed. His chest was exposed, and his arms were crossed behind his head. There was a half-smile on his face and a sultry look in his eyes. The caption read, "I'll sell your home before you get out of bed." This agent was in his first year of real estate and decided this was how he would introduce himself to the public as their agent of choice.

I don't know how many door hangers he distributed, but it was enough to create such significant blowback that many angry men and disturbed women called his brokerage to complain. The door hanger fiasco went from the "individually owned and operated" office to the cooperate headquarters in another state. It went so far up the chain that one of the senior managers of the international real estate company called the agent directly and fired him on the spot. He landed at another brokerage, and I believe he lasted a few more months before he got out of real estate altogether before his first anniversary. Years later, he's still famous in the real estate world—just not for the reasons he'd hoped.

6

MARKET YOUR BUSINESS

Marketing your business as a real estate agent is different from marketing yourself. Too often, agents try to combine the two. Before they got their real estate license, their social media pages, car, how they introduced themselves, etc., were authentically them. Then they got licensed, and their social media went from Sally to Sally the Real Estate Agent. The car got a magnet or vehicle wrap, and he wore a name tag on every outfit, no matter the occasion or plans for the day. The two became one. I'm not saying this doesn't work or won't manifest some business, but this doesn't feel consistent to me.

The goal is to create a brand for your real estate business separate from your brand. Tesla is Tesla; Elon Musk is Elon Musk. Apple is Apple; Steve Jobs was Steve Jobs. Though the two are synonymous, the person is separate from the business.

You want to promote your business as an entity and yourself as an individual. Always be thinking of the end game. If you post so much business on your personal page and then stop for a while, your clients may think you're out of business. If you don't promote your business separately, people may avoid you if you're always selling, you might become a cliché (I know that sounds harsh), and your business brand cannot gently evolve.

> You want to promote both your business as an entity and yourself as an individual.

When I joined Tara in real estate, I wasn't interested in creating a brand for myself. The entire business was focused on the name *Tara Levinson*. I still sold homes, listed properties, etc., but all the marketing was under the brand name Tara Levinson; everything said Call Tara Levinson, List with Tara Levinson, Why Work with Tara Levinson. Listing brochures, buyer consultation packets, and builder folders were all branded as Tara Levinson, regardless of who was doing the work.

Appointments would be set to list with Tara Levinson, and I would show up. Clients didn't care. Through scripting, sellers knew they were still listing with Tara Levinson. As our business grew, Tara Levinson the brand became Tara Levinson and Team, and when it grew even further, it evolved into Levinson Real Estate Team. The business name grew organically as our business grew. Her name was marketed as a brand; we didn't market the person. Marketing the brand gave greater license for creating meaningful content, advertisements, posts, etc., that engaged with the public.

If you're not new to real estate, and you've already done the one-two combo of your business and who you are, that's not a problem. It can be reworked. Think of it like this: Your mindset should be to create a business with the end goal of, "If I wasn't directly doing the work, could my business keep going?" This may never be your goal. You may never want to step out of your real estate business or grow it to that level, but this mindset will change the way you perceive and operate your business.

For example, when you—the individual—post about real estate, you're posting about your business. When you—the individual—meet someone, it's you, the individual, speaking to them. It's your job to bring up real estate through a conversation. Much different than bringing up real estate while wearing a name tag and standing in line at the grocery store.

Social media can be tricky if you don't separate yourself from your business. Most platforms work on algorithms that promote posts based on the volume of interactions, likes, comments, time spent on your post, and so on. I remember when one of my Facebook friends started selling cars. Cool. I liked and commented on his post, and maybe the next. As every post became about a car, someone he sold a car to, a new car on the lot, or him on the car lot, I interacted with his posts less and less. I flipped right past his posts because it was more of the same, and there are only so many times I can comment, "Congrats, bro." And when I interacted with his posts less and less, he disappeared from my feed. Oddly enough, he showed back up on my feed and was living in another state. I can only guess that his post about moving and pursuing personal growth had garnered so much interaction on the platform that he popped back into my feed. This is true in real life, too. If every time you met someone they went on and on about their candle business, you'd find the long way around to avoid that person in the grocery store.

Big businesses don't promote a person; they promote the business and what it does. I observed what other big companies were doing and followed their examples in marketing. I learned to create a consistent brand that's recognized by the public but is separate from myself as an individual. Because we grew our business that way, we rarely go on appointments ourselves, handle buyers individually, or do any of those types of real estate activities because our business is known locally as having the top-selling real estate agents.

We were recently buying a new car, and as we walked around the dealership, there wasn't a single person who didn't know who Tara Levinson was because of the local marketing we do. When someone asked about seeing a house, he asked if *someone* could show it to him. See what happened? She, Tara, is known as the top-selling agent. However, he knew he would

> I learned to create a consistent brand that's recognized by the public but is separate from myself as an individual.

be working with the business. No one calls Elon Musk to fix his Tesla. But Tesla is Elon Musk. Elon Musk isn't Tesla.

Do the Work

Answer these questions to build your business brand:

- **What do I want my real estate business to be known for?** This is especially important if you're looking to create a niche, such as luxury or historic properties, or as an agent serving a specific area.
- **What will my business name be?** Think with the end in mind. Will it be your name alone, a team, or a group? This is a tricky one. I teach that you should begin with the end in mind. However, calling yourself a team or group when it's only you may make you seem inauthentic. If you go this route, build a team.
- **Who's on your team?** Initially, I wanted our business to look bigger than it was, like a bird puffing out its feathers to ward

off other birds. I made it seem like the broker, relocation director, office manager, and receptionist all worked for me. In presentations, I explained how each of these roles benefited my client. Even though it was just Tara and I, I was winning listings because I had a team supporting me. Who can be on your team?

- **What logo represents my brand?** Logos make it easy for the public to identify with your business. This helps when marketing yourself because a logo can easily be added to a photo. It's a way to connect the public to your business without directly discussing it.

- **Choose colors.** You're creating a business, a company. Consistency in branding helps the public readily identify your marketing wherever it shows up. When you combine a logo, name, and colors consistently, people will begin to say, "Wow, I see you everywhere!"

- **What are your values?** Values are how you do business, and the public should know them. They should know what type of business they're working with. Your company's values should be marketed. For example, one of our values is *We Have Fun*. We did a marketing video with Santa Claus dancing in front of several new construction additions with a builder we've listed. The slogan was "Christmas in July" because the builder was doing a big giveaway. We used the extra footage and made a few *We Have Fun* value social media posts.

You either work for someone else, or you own your company. When you promote the business, you're Jane Doe promoting Jane Doe Real Estate. When we post a new listing on our business page, I will then share that post on my page. Keeping the two separate allows you to interact with your sphere without them feeling they're always in a conversation with you about real estate.

For example, when calling your sphere, separate the personal you from the business brand. A favorite script I use is:

"Hey, Bob. Do you have a moment for a business call? Great! I'm calling because I came across an investment property for sale and thought of you. Have you considered investing in rental properties?"

It's simple. If I call a friend to discuss real estate, I want them to know it's a business call. I don't want my friend to leave the conversation feeling like I used him or her. If you do that, your sphere will start to avoid your calls. Don't be the friend who has a conversation like this:

"Hey, Bob. How's it going? And the kids? I saw on Facebook that you just returned from a vacation and stayed at a VBRO. Speaking of VBROs, have you looked at investing in real estate?"

In the future, when I call to connect and don't start the conversation with "This is a business call," it can be about life. I can still ask about the VBRO but won't solicit for a sale. Just say, "I saw you rented a house. How was it?"

Events

Events are a great way to market your business. Events like the following will bring in your sphere and previous clients. Here are some that we enjoy:

- Movie night at a park or theater
- Banquets
- Margarita night
- Trick-or-treating
- Pie giveaway
- Festival of trees

What's great about marketing your business through events is that it gives you something to discuss with your business. You can post/ tie your event to your business page and interact, comment, and share from your page. That way, one event shows up on two different feeds.

A personal favorite of mine is the movie night. We did this as an annual event for years. The first year, we held it in two theaters; for our last one, we filled six theaters. People dressed up, and we had a photo backdrop at the theater. Everyone had a good time, and we kept ourselves in front of our core group.

We break down our events in quarters. During month one, we contact our database with phone calls, emails, and texts about the upcoming event. We ask if they'd like to come to the movie, get a pie, or whatever the event is. During the second month, we hold the event and contact our database about how to pick up the pie, movie tickets, etc. In the third month, we thank everyone for coming out or send them a "we missed you" message with a hint about what we're doing next.

Be sure to track your events. We use a simple spreadsheet to track who we contacted and if the pie, movie tickets, etc., were picked up. Also, keep good notes. With every event, we improve by reviewing our notes and seeing what went well and what needs improvement. Ultimately, we have created and use a standard operating procedure (SOP) for events.

Events don't have to be expensive. They can be pretty straightforward. One agent I know had her first event at her home, and she served cheese rolled up in tortillas and inexpensive wine. That's all she could afford. Her clients came. She picked up a few referrals, and now she does significant events in rented venues. Start with free, and build from there.

Advertising

Marketing your business through TV commercials, billboards, etc., can be expensive. If you don't have a strong brand in your area, a billboard or commercial is simply a stranger on a screen. These things can be added once you've built a strong brand in your market. The ROI from such expenditures is hard to track, so it's hard to know if you've been successful.

Have we used TV and billboards in our business? Yes, we have because they played into what we were trying to accomplish. For example, when we launched our independent brokerage, we used billboards to promote the independent branding of Levinson Real Estate. When the housing market went wild from 2021 to 2022, people missed out on properties because they couldn't get in to see the homes fast enough. So, we created TV commercials with the tagline, "Call today for same-day appointments."

When we wanted to become a household name in our market, we worked with a local magazine to purchase the back cover and put a real estate market update inside. We negotiated to pay for these two placements if I could add an article of my choice in every edition. We also asked the editors what would be on the front cover so we could match a house, yard, kitchen, etc., on the back to make it all look seamless. What did all this do for us? Many in our community think that's *our* magazine. So, for a fraction of the cost, a portion of the public thinks we publish a lifestyle magazine for our city.

When you invest in marketing your business, think of every possible way to use it to your advantage. Make sure you're squeezing every inch out of every dollar spent. And when it's no longer working, stop.

Get Creative

Now it's time for you to get creative regarding where you'll market the business you defined at the beginning of this section. Here are a few questions to get those creative juices flowing:

- Where am I currently marketing my business, and what are my costs?
- Where can I advertise my business for free?
- Who advocates for my business?
- Who do I want to get in front of, and where are they?

Just four questions, and then, mastermind a few more to market your business. The goal is to get in front of your database. The more you connect with your database, the more you control your business.

The Good

"I don't want to work with 'Agent's Name' anymore." It's not the best way to start a conversion with a client. Unfortunately, this wasn't the first time I'd had this conversation with a client regarding an agent on our team. I'm sure that Tara had that same conversation with one or more clients about me in the early days, though I cannot remember any such incident.

"Not a problem," I said. "I understand where you're coming from. Based on what you're telling me, I have a phenomenal agent who I think will be a better fit for you. I appreciate your honesty and continuing to trust the Levinson Real Estate Team to take care of you."

This client came to us because she'd researched our company and read the reviews, testimonials, sales history, etc. She was sold on our company's brand and wanted to work with our team to help her purchase a home. We just needed to find the right fit.

This is why separating you and your brand early is essential. If something goes wrong, it's a company issue, not a personal one.

You can remain friends with the client because it was a business issue.

The Bad

Some years back, Tara and I met a couple who did real estate together like we did. They lived in California and had similar production to us. They were great to collaborate with because they had similar growth and support staff opportunities. We kept up with each other over the years, met at conferences, and connected on Facebook.

About three years in, I noticed that they started marketing their business to the luxury crowd on Facebook. It was evident in how they dressed, the cars in their photos, and the videos of homes they created. They did a great job changing their branding from local to luxury agents. About two months into the branding change, we met at a conference, and I asked them about it.

They said they'd done well in the entry to mid-level market but wanted to break into the luxury market—to add it to their business portfolio. Sure, they sold a luxury home occasionally, but they wanted to do much more of that business. This was how they would take their production to the next level.

About a year later, we met up at another conference. I asked how their business was doing, and they said, "Terrible. Sales are way down. Our previous clients stopped working with us in our push to move into the luxury market. We noticed that we'd started slowing down but didn't know why. Then, we ran into a previous client who said they'd just sold their condo. It was a $300,000 deal. They said they would've called us but thought it was beneath us now and not worth our time. Now, we're trying to rebrand ourselves to who we were to get back our old clients."

In their pursuit of new business, the rebranding to luxury homes left their core clients behind. Could they have included the luxury market without losing the core? I think so, but it would have to be very strategic. Perhaps they could have directed at least two-thirds of their marketing to the core group and introduced a new branding for the new branch of business— such as Levinson Luxury Homes (at least that's what we did).

7

MARKET THE LISTING

Listings make real estate agents kings and queens. Regardless of the market, whether they're selling fast or sitting on the market for months, listings give you a foothold in the real estate world. However, the foothold with listings is not as strong in today's real estate market as it was twenty years ago. Third-party internet sites have come between you and the potential lead calling on one of your listings. Instead of calling the number off a sign or finding the listing on your website, most people Google the address. Up pops the paid ad for placement sites, then the third-party sites, and maybe your site will appear on page three. If you're lucky, these third-party sites may sell you back your lead, but more than likely, they've already contracted with an agent paying for that lead on your listing. This makes marketing the listing all the more critical as you work to get potential clients to call you rather than a third-party company that sells leads.

Your primary marketing goal should be to focus most of your energies on finding and marketing listings. Marketing yourself personally and your real estate business should come second because people start their home-buying search by looking for properties, not real estate agents. So why not put forth your efforts to give consumers what they're looking for, and then you can tell them how great you are?

Working with buyers is excellent, but if you're going to make the big bucks, your focus should be 75 percent on listings (getting the business and the listing itself) and 25 percent on finding buyers. And that's a conservative estimate.

> Your primary marketing goal should be to focus most of your energies on finding and marketing listings.

In a hot market, listings sell fast—in less than thirty days—and every agent wants to list houses for easy money. As I write this, most of the US is experiencing an inventory shortage. Houses are selling in days for well above the listed price. So, every agent wants the listing.

But a few years ago, I lost count of agents who said they only wanted to work with buyers. Why? Because in a market where a listing doesn't sell for four to eight months, an agent must maintain the relationship with the seller for that long and continue to invest in marketing the property. Your potential income decreases monthly as you spend more money and time trying to sell the house.

Conversely, when agents focus on creating a large listing inventory during a buyer's market, they're ahead of the game when the market shifts to a seller's market. Take our team as an example. Our listing inventory went from 130+ active homes with thirty to forty pending in early 2020 to forty to fifty active homes with ninety to one hundred pending for the next two years. Our listing inventory stayed roughly the same, but we were selling them faster than we could list them.

As the market began to cool in the summer of 2022, the numbers started to shift back to the 130+ active, with thirty to forty pending. Now, our active listing inventory goal is 200. So, when the market shifts again, we'll have more market share.

How do we do it? As I mentioned, we focus on marketing the listing. Marketing a listing is having a billboard in a neighborhood. It's the X on a treasure map, and you get to tell the world where to find the treasure. It gives you a reason to put door hangers in a neighborhood, post to social media, invite buyers to an open house, create video content, get your name out in the marketplace, and so much more. Listings let you talk about you without directly talking about you.

Very few people look for a real estate agent and then look for a house. Marketing properties online has allowed potential buyers and sellers to start looking at what's available and determining the potential price for their home months before they decide to do something. When you market a listing to its fullest potential, you get in front of these buyers and sellers.

> Listings let you talk about you without directly talking about you.

Here's a quick history lesson if you're new to real estate. When I started real estate in 2007, marketing a property quickly and cheaply was the standard practice. I still remember new listings coming across a fax machine. There's no need for great photos on a black-and-white fax. Paper flyers were still a thing; most were printed in black and white. Potential buyers wanted flyers to be available, but only about 25 to 35 percent of agents invested in flyer boxes for their listings.

The ability to search for properties online was just getting started in 2007. Realtor multi-list portals were starting to emerge, and I clearly remember taking a class on how to use the multi-list that NAR hosted in our market. Someone raised their hand and asked why we had to do this. "Let's keep to the listing books," he said. Listing books were three-ring binders where you put those faxes so other agents would know what's out there.

In those days, the multi-list portals only allowed ten low-resolution photos. I was challenged to figure out how to differentiate our listings from all the others. I would do split photos to show different angles of bathrooms and living rooms, making the ten photos stretch to fourteen or twenty. Every house we marketed had a flyer box in front. If buyers were driving around looking at properties, I wanted that flyer on their dashboard to remind them of our property.

More than that, I wanted that buyer and potential seller to be reminded of us and to see the extra steps we took beyond what other agents did. We used QR codes that took potential buyers to our website before any other agent in our market. We began using a professional photographer very early on and even hired a photographer to be on staff. Whatever edge we could find in marketing, we went after it. And we still do today.

Why am I droning on about standard or outdated marketing techniques? Because I want you to research the most innovative ways to market a listing. Anything I put in this book will likely be outdated when it's in your hands. Technology is continuously improving. So, you need to get creative in marketing your clients' listings.

How you list a property is also an advertisement to other sellers. Most sellers are also buyers. The listed home is your resume. Your goal should be to pick up at least one more listing from your current one. Your second goal is that a listed property should bring you at least two closed buyers. It would help if you were looking for a two-to-one ratio between your buyers and sellers. Have we reached that goal ourselves? Not yet. But everything we do drives us toward this goal. Do we pick up two buyers for every listing? Yes. Do we close every lead we get from a listing? Not yet. But we're working on it.

When we list a property, we follow a process designed to deliver maximum results consistently. In this chapter, we're only looking at how to market the listing to create business. I show you the list-to-closing processes in Chapter 11, which is about working with listed sellers.

Let's start doing the work of marketing your listings to create business.

Do the Work

First, don't shortcut the photos. We live in a visual world, and bad photos will keep a house from selling. Of course, you want the property to sell, and that's the apparent reason to take great photos. But the listing also serves as a resume for getting future listings. In a tough seller's market, potential sellers seek agents who stand out in marketing properties.

I've lost count of how many sellers tell me they've looked at the properties we've sold and like what we do. I love telling them to "Google us, and you will see." This works incredibly well when my competition makes bold promises about how they market a property. I say, "Have you Googled them to see if that's true?" You can't hide from the internet.

If you're working on your first listing, no worries. Go over and above it. You now have a property to use for future listing presentations. Every piece of business should work as a springboard to the next piece of business. Here are some tips that have worked for us:

- Regarding your local MLS, fill in as much information as possible. Leave no blank spaces. Leaving out information could cause a buyer to pass it by, take up unnecessary time in answering agents' questions, or a buyer may not be able to find the property in their searches.

- Be unique in your description of the home. If you constantly use the same phrases, the buyer may believe they've seen this property before.

- Change the first sentence and the front photo if a property sits on the market for over thirty days. When we list a property, we always take multiple photos of the front of the home. It often revitalizes the listing when we change the front photo and the first line of the description. A buyer who passed it by the first time may notice it now.

- Be sure to give good instructions in the agent comments. When you're easy to work with, agents will show your properties.

- Regarding social media, always have a call to action. Most agents will post to social media outside the standard of listing your property on your MLS. But that's it. Be sure to post a call to action—something, anything—to engage the public: "Call today for a same-day showing," "Ask me about the neighborhood clubhouse," "Ask for more photos," "Request a personal or video call," "Want to see the whole kitchen?" "Ask about the bonus room." Be creative in inviting the public to reach out to you.

- Get out your phone camera and create some video clips. Put your property in front of buyers and do it in an entertaining way. Sites like TikTok and Instagram offer free video editing tools to make your house look and sound like a music video or something much more interesting than, "Here's a fireplace; there's a kitchen." Having someone edit a video like this for your property used to cost a lot of money. With a basic tutorial, you can do it for free.

- Create a separate video to sell the property and one to sell you as an agent. Avoid videos that make fun of agents or clients. They may be funny and get other agents to like your videos, but how do you think the public perceives them?
- Don't worry about being perfect—do it! Doing something consistently over time breeds results and skills. You'll only get better by executing the skill. Just start making videos of your listings.

Get Active!

Don't be afraid to knock on a few doors to get directly in front of the public. You have a great reason to reach out now that you have a great listing. It's as simple as:

> *Script*: *"Hello, I'm with (your team/brokerage). I just listed (seller's name) (home/house) down the street at (address). I wanted to introduce myself because I'll be working to get their home sold. By chance, do you know anyone who's been wanting to move into the neighborhood?"*

Notice two things: First, the script uses the seller's name. It makes it personal. Neighbors are personal. Second, there's a call to action: "Do you know someone who wants to move to the neighborhood?"

Should you still do flyers? It's up to you. If I had only one or two listings, I would. I use every tool to pick up buyers and show potential sellers what I do. During COVID-19, we stopped doing flyers because we weren't sure if people would take them. Most, if not all, agents in our area did the same. As I write this, I'm thinking about adding flyers to a few of our listings to see if it creates more buyer leads as the market shifts.

We currently use "Text for Info" signs for all our listings, and they directly feed into our database and distribute to our team. I saw a study that said buyers are more likely to respond to an additional sign other than the For Sale sign, so we use a corrugated one-by-two-foot sign that we put next to our real estate sign.

Work the open house. Look back at Chapter 1 for all those details. I'd only add that you should work those open houses for leads. If the property is overpriced, make it a buyer farm. Work it every Sunday if it's the only listing you have. If you have no other appointments scheduled, what else will you do? If you think you need a day off, then pick another day. I'm a six-days-a-week kind of person. I know someone so much better than me who only rested on the seventh day.

Invite the public if you decide to do a broker's open house. If you take the time and invest capital into inviting other agents to view the home, why not invite the public, too? We use this strategy at every broker's open. We put an open house sign in the yard to advertise it and typically send mailers throughout the neighborhood. This is another door-knocking opportunity.

> ***Script***: *"Hello, my name is (name), with (brokerage). This Thursday from 4:00 p.m. to 6:00 p.m., we're holding a broker's open house at (seller's names) house. We'll be serving (food/drinks) and would love for you to stop by. If you know anyone who may want to move to the neighborhood, please invite them."*

Are broker's open houses a waste of time? Maybe, if you don't invite the public—unless there's something unique about the house. For example, we had a listing that didn't photograph well. No matter what angle we used, the floor plan didn't make sense in the photos. We held a twilight broker's open from 4:00 p.m. to 6:00 p.m. and made it a happy-hour party and lots of agents showed up. This increased the traffic to the house, which led to a buyer. Success! We also picked up a seller and a few buyers by inviting the public to attend. Again, success!

A broker's open house lets you be creative, get agents to the property, and make it fun for the public. Another time, we partnered with a local suit store, and they did a mini-fashion show of the latest fall fashions. This brought out a lot of agents, and the store owner invited his clients to the event, so I got to meet them. A win for everyone.

Generating leads is so much simpler when you provide something of value. Remember that the goal is to sell the house, but if that house doesn't meet their needs, you can find another.

Now that you have a few things to do with your listing, get to it.

The Good

You're not the only one who represents you; the people who work for you also represent you and what you stand for. I received a call from a builder who said he wanted to list all his properties. I scheduled an appointment to meet with him the next day, did my research, and prepared for the presentation.

When we met, I asked him a series of questions to learn more about him and his business so I could tailor what we do for him. Questions such as:

- How long have you been building?
- What led you to become a builder?
- What are your goals for this year in terms of homes built?
- Are you looking to scale your business?
- What are a few of your favorite features about the homes you build?

From there, I showed him what we would do. He stopped me mid-presentation and said, "I'm going to list with you. I don't need you to show me everything you do. I'm sure it's all top notch. The other day, I was sitting in my truck in front of one of my houses. I saw someone who I assumed works for you. She pulled up to the house and put flyers in the box. Then, she returned to her truck, pulled some paper towels, and cleaned the sign. If your people take the initiative to do that, I know everything else is just as great."

A simple act of making sure we always look the best won us a builder with multiple listings. What are your expectations for yourself and your team?

The Bad

Be careful about what you become known for with your listings. An agent friend told me how he'd listed a property in a neighborhood to get a foothold in that addition. It was an affluent housing addition with over three times our market average sales price. He agreed to work for a very reduced commission to win the first listing. He told the seller that this was a special deal just for him. He did a great job listing the property and went above and beyond—going so far as to personally clean the seller's pool when it was green with algae.

That seller was so thankful for all his hard work and the great deal he got that he told a neighbor, who told a neighbor, who told a neighbor, and so on. He listed many properties in that neighborhood, but they were all for that reduced commission, which meant he had to do a lot of additional stuff to sell those houses. He eventually stopped listing properties there. It got too expensive and was too much work. After all, anyone who didn't get the great deal and the above-and-beyond service felt slighted. If you do it once, be prepared to do it repeatedly.

8

FARMING

Farming is just what it sounds like. It's working on a particular area over some time to get results. Like farming for fruit or vegetables, farming for leads takes cultivation and time. It can cost you a lot of money or time or fall somewhere in between. It means becoming a constant with a particular group. You create the narrative for them depending on your marketing goals. You become the face of a real person in their mailbox or on a door hanger. You become ever-present.

Farming aims to create clients from desired areas or demographics so you can grow your business where you want it to grow. Ideally, you'll start where people already know you, like the area where you live or where you've already sold one or more homes. The most accessible new business is always with people who know you or are currently working with you. If you want to move into a new market, such as luxury homes (a market) or downtown condos (an area) and don't yet have a foothold, you must employ creative marketing.

For example, in 2010, three condo developments had been for sale for roughly two years, and very few units were sold. The developments started in 2007, and the market went through the floor in 2008. We met with the developers, pitched our marketing plan, and won the business. We planned to market the properties, of course. They'd previously been on our local MLS, but that was about it. Downtown luxury condos were a new thing in

> Farming aims to create clients from desired areas or demographics, so you can grow your business where you want it to grow.

the Oklahoma City market. The public noticed them but didn't understand why someone would want to live in a small condo when they could live in a house with a yard.

After extensive research, we created an in-depth plan to saturate the market with information and lifestyle marketing built around the condo developments. Our second goal was to make Tara Levinson, the lead listing agent, downtown famous. The farming strategy was to market the property *and* market the agent.

We began to market Tara as the go-to for downtown properties and targeted downtown businesses where people worked but didn't live. We peppered them with Tara's information about how to enjoy "Bricktown Living." (Bricktown was what the condos were called at the time.)

As long as we continued to work in that area of business, we had that area of business. But when we shifted our focus to other areas, we got less and less of the downtown business. We still sell in the downtown area, but not at the level we once did. Other agents have moved in and taken over the downtown area through their farming and our lack of it. We strategically shifted our farming strategy to different areas that align with our overall brand and strategies.

Do the Work

Now it's time to work on specific, actionable items you can do to farm specific areas, market to your database, and grow your business.

I've already mentioned door-knocking a few times. You may be thinking, *Oh, please! Not again.* I will talk about knocking on doors again because it's free. If you have no money to invest in passive marketing strategies like mailers or door hangers (both of which we'll discuss in a bit), then door-knocking is something you can do to grow your business. If you have the nerve to knock on a stranger's door and introduce yourself, everything else in real estate is downhill. If you're not good at knocking on doors initially, keep doing it. You'll improve and develop more confidence in this and other real estate strategies.

A simple script you can use when knocking on doors is:

Script: *"Hello, my name is (name) with (brokerage).I live at (address or just general area). I just wanted to take a moment and introduce myself to my neighbors. Since I live in the area, please feel free to reach out if you ever have any real estate needs. Since I live here, I know this market very well."*

See how simple this is? If you don't like this script, modify it to make it your own. Just introduce yourself, let them know you're in real estate, and offer something of value. Always create value within your sphere.

Using door hangers is another way to farm an area. Note of caution: Since they are door hangers, hang them on a door. Don't put them in mailboxes. Mailboxes are only for mail with postage. As a broker, I've had my fair share of angry neighbors who told me it's illegal for my agents to put items in their mailbox without going through the postal service. So don't do it. Get a door hanger and put it on the door.

When designing your door hanger, I have a couple of suggestions. If the point is to market *you*, follow the same pattern you use when creating a script: introduce yourself, let them know you're in real estate, and offer something of value. If you're marketing a *property*, we've designed a few generic door hangers that can be used for multiple properties—one for new listings, one for open houses, and one for just-sold properties. The door hangers contain our general information (name, phone number, email address, scannable barcode website, and some graphics). There's also a blank text box where we manually write in the property address. This is the most inexpensive way to produce door hangers because you can mass print a large quantity for a much lower cost than printing individual door hangers for each property.

Mailers are a little more expensive form of marketing than knocking on doors or producing door hangers because of the cost of postage. Furthermore, you must commit that you won't give up after one or two mailings. Consistency over time breeds results, and this is especially true for mailers. If you only mail once or twice, your postcard or letter is a quick toss in the trash for prospective clients. It takes consistency over time for the public to finally wonder, *Who is this person who keeps mailing me stuff?*

Hand-written cards are the best for client engagement. If you don't have time and your finances permit, I recommend going with a company that sends cards that look/are handwritten. There are several of them in the marketplace. A handwritten note, even a computer-generated note that looks handwritten, shows more sincerity and authenticity to the client. Beyond birthday or holiday cards, you can send a market analysis, just-listed properties, just-sold properties, open houses, market stats, and neighborhood updates. Remember that farming aims to work an area consistently over time. So be consistent and keep working it over time.

Social media fosters a whole new area of farming. Join local neighborhood pages or Facebook groups and be active by commenting, interacting, and posting. This is how you can stay in front of your potential clients while adding value. Don't just pop up with, "I sell real estate. Who needs a market analysis?" Instead, engage with others in the group.

Be sure to check out levinsonedu.com/prep for various farming examples.

The Good

Tara and I sat at the dining room table after walking through the property. As we asked the owners our standard listing questions, we came to the one that said, "What led you to reach out to our team for the sale of your house?" Tara had been the listing agent when the house was sold several years ago, but she didn't remember this couple.

To answer the question, the wife walked to the fridge and took our business card off the door. Then she opened her purse and took out two or three more of our business cards.

When she sat at the table again, she said, "We bought this house several years ago. You weren't our real estate agent. You were the agent for the sellers. You started mailing me a few months after we moved in—simple letters about our house and homes sold in the area. That sort of stuff. At first, I threw the cards away. You weren't our agent, so why keep them? But you kept sending us stuff, and our agent never did. Eventually, I felt guilty and started tossing them in my purse and handing them out when someone said they needed an agent. So, when we decided to sell, we called you."

I almost fell out of my chair. This wonderful lady kept our cards, handed them out, and told people about us. Her agent had failed to keep up with her, but we did and won her over. We call the buyers of our listings orphans because they're often forgotten after the transaction is complete. I've heard it said that upward of 76 percent of people would use their agent again to purchase a home. But some agents don't stay in front of their clients and lose the business to someone else who does.

The Bad

Remember the overly sexualized door hanger that cost an agent his real estate career? This was an example of a farming strategy that was poorly thought out. No need to rehash that scenario again, but I will tell on myself. Remember how I told you we took over and dominated our downtown market? We used mailers, door hangers, and three banners that hung on the side of the buildings that were like billboards that folks could see while driving downtown. We were involved in roughly 75 percent of all downtown transactions in three years.

We even officed downtown out of one of the townhomes for sale. We moved a few miles north when we sold the building where we officed. We continued to sell more homes every year, but we stopped marketing to the downtown area. Other agents moved in, opened their brokerages, and created billboards. Years later, we occasionally sell a few properties in that area, but it's less than 2 percent of our sales. We worked hard to pave the way and let the business go—what a waste.

We've also made the mistake of not being consistent with our farming. We've sent out "just listed" or "just sold" cards several times in an area with no results, then decided that farming doesn't work. Of course, that type of farming doesn't work; it's equal to throwing out tomato seeds once or twice and wondering why you don't have tomatoes. To have a tomato garden, you must work the garden. To have leads in an area, you must consistently work there.

Please don't make the same mistakes we made. Learn from our marketing failures to successfully farm and consistently gain new clients.

PART 2

I HAVE A LEAD –
NOW WHAT?

9

LEADS AND TYPES OF CLIENTS

I t was our new agent's first week. He was handling incoming calls, and I sat at a desk on the other side of the room. At that time, our office was a communal, open-spaced room with desks sprinkled throughout, which was bad for having a private conversation but good for listening to new agents work the phones. After a twenty-minute call, the new agent set an appointment to meet the client at the house.

He turned to me with a big smile and said, "How was that?"

I momentarily looked at him to gather my thoughts and replied, "Great job asking for the appointment and not giving up. But that was, by far, the worst agent-to-potential-client conversation I've ever heard."

What was so bad? Most of what he said was completely fabricated. He made up a nonsensical response if he didn't know the answer. An appointment was set, but we never heard from the lead again. I'm pretty sure that after his conversation, that lead was more confused than before they called.

Today, that agent is still a core member of our team, a close friend, and a leader in scripting and training in our office. I learned a valuable lesson that morning. When an agent finally gets that call, that lead must know what to do afterward.

> Answering the phone, the right scripts, and following systems and processes create success when your lead-generation efforts connect you with a prospective client.

The first step is understanding what the lead (the person calling) wants from you. The second step is to know the proper script to address that need.

Answering the phone, the right scripts, and following systems and processes create success when your lead-generation efforts connect you with a prospective client.

A, B, and C Buyers/Sellers

You can classify your clients into three categories based on how ready, willing, and able they are to list or buy a property.

- Category A clients are clients you've set an **A**ppointment with.
- Buyers who haven't set an appointment are on the **B**ench and are the B clients.
- The rest are C clients, meaning you have some **C**hallenges to overcome before they buy or sell with you.

Your mindset must be that everyone at some point in time will be ready, willing, and able to buy or sell if you set the appointment or overcome the challenge. You determine if someone is an A buyer or a B buyer. You can always keep your clients in the A category by never leaving one appointment without setting a time for the next appointment when you'll show them properties again.

This does two things. First, it gives you a deadline to find more properties to view. Second, it gives them a predetermined time to view more properties. And if they come across something they want to see on their own, they can let you know so you can arrange a viewing. When making the appointment to meet again, say, "If you come across any properties you'd like to see before we meet, let me know. I can set them up, or if we need to see it sooner, we can do that."

Setting appointments also applies to listing clients. Don't leave the property until you set the next appointment. It could be when the photographer comes out, when they can expect the property to be live, or when the first open house will be scheduled. It's about creating an expectation and meeting that expectation. Sellers want to feel there's always forward momentum (and there should be), and continually setting the next appointment helps create that.

If you have what could be an A buyer and don't set an appointment, guess what? You just put them on the bench. If you keep them on the bench long enough, they'll set an appointment with another agent. Ready, willing, and able clients won't wait for you to find a house for them. From sites like Zillow to Facebook, buyers and sellers continually see homes on the market; that's precisely where they're looking. And every one of those houses has a listing agent they can call.

Clients in the C category have a challenge you need to overcome. Notice I said, "You need to overcome." Maybe the seller needs to do some home improvements or repairs before the property can be listed. How can you ensure they're being done and you're still top of mind when the property is ready to list? Connect the seller with contractors and stop by to see what has been completed. Use this as an opportunity to build rapport with the client.

If the buyer has a low credit rating, check with them to see how they are hitting their milestones toward raising their credit score. Set up a time to view a few properties now and then to whet their appetites.

When a client purchases a property, they go from A client to a C client. Your challenge now is to maintain the relationship so when they are again ready, willing, and able to buy or sell, you're the one who sets the appointment. It's a challenge that may take years to overcome, but it's your challenge to do so. According to the National Association of Realtors, 74 percent of sellers said they'd work with the same agent to sell again. Yet only 26 percent of them did so. That means roughly 48 percent of agents didn't overcome the challenge of keeping up with their clients to move them from C to A clients.

Listings create kings and queens in real estate. Without listings to market, real estate agents are in a spiral of paying fees for internet leads, or they must find sources for buyer leads. Listings give you a foothold in the real estate business. Too many agents rely on buyer leads, especially buyer leads they pay for. Whether it's from a referral fee or a paid buyer lead, unless you have the listing, your business is at the mercy of the market and the company that holds the leads.

10

SELLER LEADS

S eller leads put you in control of the market, meaning another company doesn't decide your business success and income. Listings allow an agent to market the property on various real estate websites, put signs in the yard that get your name out, and create social media posts, mailers, etc. Buyers look first for properties, then for a real estate agent. If you have a listing, you have what a buyer wants.

When we began working together, one of my coaching clients was grossing more than $300,000 a year in commissions. But he was spending over $17,000 monthly for many buyer leads. Within six months, that number was around $5,000 a month in internet leads. We focused on finding listings and then maximized his activities around those listings. He gained control of his business and was more in control of his income.

When I started in real estate, I was heavily focused on working with relocation businesses. Associating with them brought us leads to work, but all the additional reports and updates they required kept us extremely busy and under the thumb of the company. Since we worked with so many relocation companies, when a client returned to us to purchase their next home, they pressured us to put them back through the system. Even though we'd kept up with our sphere to create a returning opportunity, the relocation company thought we should pay them a referral fee, even though the second opportunity to sell to the client didn't come through them.

This may or may not still be the case. We haven't worked on that part of the real estate business since 2009 because I realized we could do one-third of the business and make the same money by heavily focusing on finding seller leads and working every aspect of that lead to create additional business. Conversely, we gained back two-thirds of our time because we didn't have to do all those reports.

Now, one of the primary gauges of the health of our business is our listing inventory. Having listings gives us confidence that we'll see consistent business year over year as we work our database. We control the success of our business by focusing on finding seller leads. Following this strategy, you can have that same consistency in your business that doesn't rely on another company to create momentum for you.

Do the Work

When someone tells you they have a home that they want to sell, set the appointment. And set the appointment as soon as possible. You may be reading this with an *Of course!* mentality. However, too many agents create roadblocks by not setting the appointment immediately. If you wait, another agent will pressure the seller to list with them.

Agent: *"Are you available to meet this afternoon at 3:30 p.m. or 5:00 p.m.?"*

Seller: *"Well, my spouse doesn't get off work until 5:00 p.m."*

Agent: *"No problem. If he's off at 5:00, let's meet at 6:00. This will give him time to get home and unwind before I arrive. Does that work better for you?"*

If that feels too straightforward for you, then ask:

"When would be a good time for me to come by and walk through the property so I can give you an accurate listing price for your house?"

I prefer the straight-to-it scripts. Not because I have an overbearing or dominant personality, but when you name specific times to meet, you make it easier for clients than if you said, "When is the best time for you?" You'll set the appointment much earlier, and your clients will feel more confident in you.

When working with buyers, always use the word *home.* But when working with sellers, use the word *house.* This encourages them to start emotionally detaching from their property and will help during the negotiations when you receive an offer or are working through repair requests. People are more willing to sell their houses than their homes.

You may hear the objection:

"We aren't ready for anyone to walk through yet. We need to take care of a few things before we're ready to sell."

A simple scripted response is to say:

"That's all the more reason for me to come out. Sometimes, you need to spend less than you think before a house is ready to sell. You may not need to put more in your house before you can get out of your house."

When preparing for an appointment, I like pulling the data I need to win a listing presentation and having a printed copies of the data, everything I can find. Yes, I print out the data. I would rather have material ready to share than not have an answer to a question. I print out the data. Yes, technology is excellent, and everything digital is fantastic, but printed copies carry more weight than digital reports when speaking numbers and statistics. Save the digital for examples of marketing. If you still decide to go digital, no problem. Just be sure to have a paper copy as backup. There's nothing worse than having your tech fail at the dining room table when presenting to a potential client.

Always start with touring the home. After all, how can you give an accurate assessment of the value of a property without first viewing the home? I have a tested strategy for the home tour. I recommend you start in the master bedroom. You're a stranger in their home so that in itself is uncomfortable. Second, the most private room in a home is the master bedroom. The more comfortable rooms tend to be the dining or living rooms, where people usually gather. So, start in the most uncomfortable room, and while walking through the house, create rapport with the owners while learning about the house. When you make it to the dining room table, they'll be comfortable with you and in a comfortable space.

> I recommend you start in the master bedroom.

If you start in the living room, the sellers will start with being uncomfortable with a stranger walking through their home and finish with only being slightly *more* uncomfortable because you're in their master bedroom—a very private space. What they'll remember, along with only about 50 percent of what you discussed, is that they felt uncomfortable with you. Consciously or subconsciously, it will be there.

Don't Talk Numbers Yet

Don't fall into the trap of, "Let's discuss the commission before we do the walk-through" or, "Let's talk about what you can sell the house for before we walk through."

You don't want to immediately start talking numbers because you need to give yourself time to create rapport and emphasize the value of what you do. The sellers are in a state of logical motivation. Does it make financial sense to work with you? You need to uncover the emotional motivations that created their logical motivations. The walk-through gives you those opportunities.

The conversations can be as simple as:

Seller: *"Let's discuss your commission before we do the walk-through."*

Agent: *"Before I can properly discuss what it will take to sell your home, such as my marketing investments, I need to be able to see the house and determine an accurate value. Let's start in the master bedroom."*

Or

Seller: *"Before we walk through, let's talk about the price you can sell the house for."*

Agent: *"I have an idea of the price from the statistical research I've done, but I need to validate my analysis by walking through the house before I can give you an accurate value. I prefer to start in the primary bedroom and work our way around the house. Which way is that?"*

Discovering the seller's motivation keeps the client from listing to contract to closing. I have and will mention this multiple times, but people tend to make decisions out of emotion and validate those decisions with logic. So, you'll need to know your client's emotional and logical motivations. By asking questions during the listing presentation, you can take what you learn about their emotional and logical motivations and apply market data to connect emotional and logical reasoning. When you speak about the market, you speak the language of real estate. You'll need to use tie-down statements to connect the motivations to the market to win the listing. To recap:

- Discover the emotional motivations.
- Find out the logical motivations.
- Speak the language of real estate.
- Incorporate tie-down statements.

Questions to uncover emotional motivations:

- Would you mind telling me why you want to move?
- What would you say are your goals in selling?
- What led you to decide to put your house on the market?
- When your house sells, what's the next step for you?

Countless follow-up questions can be written to those four simple questions. Remember, your goal is to discover their motivation and how they justified the decision to sell.

It would help if you learned to ask great questions. I will give you a statement, and I invite you to write/think of as many questions as possible that could have led to making the following statement.

> *"Based on what you're telling me, you want to find a home where your family can grow but also have room for family and friends to stay with you. And you're hoping to be able to sell to have enough in equity to put 20 percent down on your next home and still have enough left over."*

Here's another one:

> *"Your goal is to have your home on the market in the next thirty days and sold in November so your whole family can be together in Denver by Christmas."*

Throughout this book, I give you example questions, but more importantly, I want to teach you to think of your own questions. When you learn to ask questions, you'll be a master salesman.

One of the most important questions you can ask a seller is,

"What price do you want to sell your home for?"

Never fall for,

"I don't know. That's why you're here."

They know. Sellers always have an idea of what price they want to sell for. So, keep asking the question until they tell you. Counter the conversation above with:

Agent: *"Absolutely, but when you were thinking about selling, what price did you have in mind?"*

Seller: *"Oh, we didn't think about it."*

Agent: *"But what would you like to net if your home did sell?"*

Seller: *"We would like to net about $20,000."*

Agent: *"And what do you currently owe on your mortgage?"*

One time, I asked the question in one form or another seven times before the sellers told me what they wanted to net/sell for. The sellers had an emotional motivation that caused them to want to sell, and they validated their emotional motivation by logically stating to themselves that if they sold/made this much, it would be worth it and would meet their goals.

After you know what the seller wants, using market statistics and calculating closing costs—along with a seller net price—you can use a tie-down statement such as:

"Based on the value of your home, it looks like we can list at $325,000, with a possible sale at $320,000. That would net you $10,000 above your goal of $30,000. How does that sound? . . . Fantastic, I can have my photographer here at noon tomorrow for photographs. Does that time work for you?"

Conversations around commission are easily navigated with a seller's net sheet. Suppose the sellers meet their goals, emotional motivations, and logical motivations. In that case, you can refer to the net sheet showing that your commission is already figured into their net at closing. They get what they want (or more) at your charge rate.

From there, you can begin the listing paperwork. Do it right there at the table. Everything goes back to "always set the appointment." You don't need to ask, "Would you like to list your house with me?" Just set the next appointment that moves the listing along and start the paperwork.

The Good

Sometimes, the best listings are the ones that don't sell. I know that doesn't sound good, but stay with me here. Your duty as an agent who *lists* a property is to *sell* that property. Every effort should be made to sell it. Yet, once in a blue moon, a property comes along that won't sell, but everyone calls on it. Maybe the floor plan is terrible, the remodel was done wrong, or the location is horrible—whatever the case may be, everyone wants to see it, but no one wants to buy it. You've found yourself a buyer's garden. Keep marketing that house to the best of your ability, and for every lead you get, be sure to have backup houses to show if they don't want that one.

We once had a property that would not sell. We had it on the market for over a year. The house was a beast to get under contract and keep under contract. From marketing that house, which eventually sold, we created over thirty additional buy-side transactions. We lost count of the number of calls we received. We once joked about making the house a lead source category on our P&L.

Did you notice I said it took over a year to sell? Yes, it did, and the clients stayed happy with us throughout the listing period because we followed our systems and processes.

The Bad

When working with builders, the first deal will be the best. I put this story under *The Bad* to illustrate that working with builder-sellers can be unique. However, understand that whatever original agreement is made between the services you'll provide and the commission you'll earn, this will be the best the agreement will ever be for you. The builder will want you to do more—and do it for less—as time progresses and you list more and more of the builder's properties.

Keep in mind you're selling that builder's product, which means you fall under the debt section of their P&L. If a builder can figure out how to reduce the debt side of their P&L, they will. If a builder isn't good at controlling their expenses, it's not uncommon for you, the agent, to net more than the builder when all is said and done. That leaves a bad taste in the builder's mouth, and two things will happen. Either they'll find someone to do it cheaper or want more from you. Either way, your income goes down.

When we moved brokerages, a couple was the number one selling team at the brokerage and one of the top teams in the state. They were one of the first in our area to break the million dollars in GCI ceiling (considering average sales prices were less than $220,000 at that time). Accolades and applause followed them around the office and at conferences. They were invited to the inner circle of many realtor mastermind groups. Then, out of the blue, the builder took his business in-house and away from this couple. They went from the top to the bottom to out of sight. Every aspect of their business was tied up with this one builder. When he went away, their business went away.

The moral of the story is that if you work with builders, don't rely on them for your business. Treat them as clients, but work the business like a referral source, and milk everything you can from the marketing and leads that come in. Feed your database and stay in touch with them. When they sell, be sure they call you back to be their agent.

11

WORKING WITH LISTED SELLERS

The paperwork is complete; the marketing is in place, and the sign is in the yard. Now, the real work begins. Once you have the listing, the work doesn't stop there. Like a buyer who still needs to find a house, your seller needs to sell the house. The goal is to meet your client's goals and create income for yourself.

As long as the house is on the market, it's attracting potential new buyers to the property. Plus, you have the added benefit of continuing to work with the listed seller. There is no more significant source of new business than your current business. Keeping a seller informed and happy can create tremendous benefits for you. It's your opportunity to create clients for life, whether the property sells quickly or you maintain the listing for an extended time.

Markets flow between seller's markets and buyer's markets. When I entered real estate at the end of 2007, the market shifted nationally to a buyer's market. From 2020 to early 2022, we had the most robust seller's market ever seen. No matter the market, the systems and processes we use to take care of our sellers cannot change. How you market your listings cannot change. Maintaining consistency in your systems and processes creates clients for life and establishes your brand.

Below, we'll explore various systems and processes regarding weekly updates, vacation property checks, market updates, price reduction scripts, and other to-do items. They are all designed to keep your seller from looking out their front window at the real estate sign and wondering if their agent thinks about them as much as they do about her. Early in my career, I asked clients what frustrated them most about their real estate experience. Most sellers said that after they listed their house, they never heard from their agent again. Don't let that be you.

> Most sellers said that after they listed their house, they never heard from their agent again. Don't let that be you.

When you list a property, there's the initial excitement of your potential income. After a week or so goes by and the property hasn't sold, hitting the "next" button could be tempting to look for more business. There's no need to look elsewhere. When you create systems and processes for marketing properties and keep your sellers updated, they stay happy and informed. When they're happy, they refer others to you.

In 2020, when the market heated up, many agents stopped marketing themselves or their properties. Their monthly newsletters stopped going out, social media posts became fewer, and less was invested in property marketing, etc. Properties were selling quickly, so agents didn't see a need for all that.

Our business has grown because our systems and processes remain the same regardless of market conditions. Using the listing to farm for new buyers hasn't changed. Keeping our sellers informed and working to sell the property hasn't changed. Consistency is vital to the year-over-year growth we continue to enjoy.

When I say our systems haven't changed, I don't mean we neglect to improve things. One of our core values is "We embrace change and drive innovation." This is a core reason why overall real estate sales improved by 10 percent during the seller's market, and our team's sales improved by 33 percent.

Many agents think they're doing better when simply riding the market's rising tide. They cut back on their marketing, or they cut corners on marketing a property because it sells quickly, and they don't need to market it. Buyers are everywhere in a seller's market, so why waste time and money on things like marketing yourself?

When our local market began to shift with rising interest rates in 2022, agents said, "The market is slowing down." The market was slowing in the first and second quarters, and instead of twenty people trying to buy the same property, there were three or four people. The number of showings slowed down on properties, but homes still sold in about the same amount of time for almost the same price.

Agents who found their business was slowing down began posting about a shifting market. But the market hadn't shifted yet. Statistically, sales were on par with what they were the year before. But the activity level had dropped, and agents who'd stopped marketing themselves tried to become relevant again. Newsletters started back up, and social media posts reappeared in an attempt to create business.

Don't be those agents. Be consistent in all that you do. Consistency breeds good business.

Do the Work

In Chapter 7, we discussed ways to find buyers. This section touches on a few more marketing practices and basic systems and processes to keep the client happy over an extended period.

Let's start with a process that begins when you take a listing. The following activities are involved:

1. The listing paperwork is completed.
2. Photos, video, and VR tour are completed within twenty-four hours of completing the listing paperwork.
3. Property is listed.
4. Send links to the seller for review.
5. Send links to agents/team members to review.
6. Upload walk-through notes with listing paperwork.

1. Listing Paperwork Completed: You may think, *I will do that!* I'll beat this drum a little louder in Chapter 21 about knowing the contracts and documentation. Let me say this: Be sure to follow your broker's checklist before listing and get everything signed and disclosed when you're supposed to. When it comes to failure to follow the rules/laws of contracts and documentation, it's not a problem until it's a problem. Then, it's a big problem.

2. Photos, video, and VR tour completed within twenty-four hours. Luxury homes will take a little longer, but we've always aimed to have everything up and running within twenty-four hours. This creates a *Wow!* factor with clients, protecting you from the seller saying, "I have a buyer for my house" before it's officially marketed. Darn—you have a listing contract, and now they don't want to be in contract with you. That doesn't happen often, but it does happen.

3. Property is listed. Ensure the property appears on all the real estate sites the seller expects it to be on. Be sure that all the appropriate information is uploaded. You need to check the online listings first to catch any errors, such as if the property's location is incorrect on the map. You want to be proactive versus reactive, which takes us to step four.

4. Send links to the seller for review. This is one of my favorite steps because I get to say:

> *"I've only been in your house a few times, but you live there daily. Please review the marketing to ensure it meets your expectations."*

When you have their approval, and it doesn't sell right away, you've removed any finger-pointing that could occur about the marketing. The seller told you it met their expectations. And if a mistake was made, they'll find it and let you know. When you engage the seller in the process, they feel like they're on your team to sell their house, and that's an excellent place for a seller to be. They're working with you to sell their house.

5. Send links to agents/team members to review. If you have a team, share the links with them so they can review the property to see if it meets their buyers' needs. Share the links with other agents in other brokerages. Create a relationship with other agents where you send them your listings, and they share theirs. Learn to work together with other agents.

6. Upload walk-through notes with listing paperwork. Never trust yourself to remember everything. You took the time to write notes during the initial walk-through, so keep them somewhere safe, like where you keep the listing paperwork. I also upload my entire listing presentation, so I have everything I've shared with them available for reference if I ever need it.

Keep the Seller Informed

Now, you know the six basic steps to list a property. With that, let's move into what to do from the second week forward: Always keep the seller informed about everything you're doing.

Always create daily value with your clients. One way to do this is to call your sellers every week—no exceptions. They see your real estate sign every day. In their yard is a daily reminder of your success or failure. When sellers are frustrated that their house hasn't sold, they're even more frustrated if you don't call them. So, call them and add value. Set a designated time when you'll send them a weekly update.

I build a basic weekly update script that can be customized for each seller. It could be an overall market analysis, discuss upcoming holidays or local events that may affect the market, etc, such as the following email script examples:

"As the holiday season approaches, the number of showings typically decreases. However, the showings that do happen are true buyers who are interested in your house. Last year, we saw _____ homes sell in the month of _____. So homes do sell during the holidays."

"It's not uncommon for showings to decrease during an election period because there's always a little uncertainty. Now that we've moved through the election time, I expect to see a bit of an increase in traffic."

"Since your property came on the market _____ weeks ago, we've seen _____ homes go under contract. I don't know the specifics of the properties still pending, but I'll find out if and when they close. The differences between your house and these houses are. . ."

In the last email template, you tell your clients about the properties that have already sold or gone under contract. More than likely, your sellers already know about them. Don't wait for them to ask you about them—that puts you in a defensive position. Always be proactive.

Have you heard of the accusations audit that Chris Voss shares in his book *Never Split the Difference*—the best book I've ever read about negotiating? The accusations audit is where you essentially tell on yourself. By admitting them first, you remove all the negative things someone could say about you. This is how you can be proactive in shaping the narrative versus reactive, where you must respond to someone else's agenda. Whether you're in a seller's or buyer's market, you want to control the narrative with your clients as much as possible.

It's also essential to control your time with sellers without them feeling like you're unavailable. One way to control your time is through weekly email updates and phone calls. If you call them, it reduces the chances of them calling you with questions. Another way to control your items is the following simple script:

> *"If I receive an offer or come across something that cannot wait until the morning, can I contact you after 7:00 p.m.?"*

This implies that you won't call them after 7:00 p.m. unless it's crucial. That you respect their time and hope they'll respect yours. It's a way of saying, "Don't call me all hours of the night," without saying, "Out of respect for my family, I won't answer my phone after 7:00 p.m."

As your real estate career progresses, you'll add to these systems and processes (SOPs). You'll get better and create more in-depth SOPs based on how you do business. And that's how it should be.

Final thought: Doing something the right way takes time; doing it the wrong way takes even more time.

The Good

"You aren't going to fire me, are you?" the seller asked. The property had been on the market for almost a year. We'd consistently held open houses, sent market updates, coordinated repairs based on feedback, and checked on the property when the owner went on vacation, but the home had not sold. A few offers had come in that were more aggressive than the sellers wanted to accept. This may have added to their guilt about the work we'd put in.

From a financial standpoint, we were already in the red in terms of a return on investment on our commissions when the property did sell—only looking at the sale of the property and not the buyer and seller leads we picked up during the marketing of the property. We had a billboard in the neighborhood that brought another listing, numerous sign calls that we converted to buyers, and held an open house at the property every third week, bringing in buyer leads. Not to mention, because the seller felt guilty about the amount of work we were putting in, they referred us any time someone needed to sell or buy. As I've repeatedly said, "Your success in real estate is directly proportional to the number of people who when they think of real estate, they think of you."

"No, we aren't firing you," I said. "We're going to sell your house." And we did.

The Bad

Sometimes, people aren't happy no matter what you do. You can send weekly updates, have verbal conversations, and present offers. And yet, the seller is just not happy.

I was working with a seller, and he'd been receiving my weekly updates regarding his property. At this time in our market, houses sat on the market for about sixty days with an inventory between five and six months. And they typically sold for below list price with closing costs paid by the seller. His weekly update included a recap showing feedback, market analysis for his neighborhood, and a general look at the market. About four weeks into the listing, I did my follow-up call. In an angry tone, he said, "The weekly updates you're sending me don't have enough data. I expect a more in-depth market review to see why my house hasn't sold. I work in investigations, and information is how things are solved. Where's the data and information?" Of course, he didn't mention the few offers we'd received on his house that he'd rejected.

Based on this phone call, I went all out with the details. And I mean all out. The update had charts, graphs, and data galore. I pulled data for him on every site where we marketed his property so he could see the most minute details about his property.

Two weeks after this, I received another angry phone call. "Why am I getting these long email updates? I want a basic update on what is active, pending, or sold in my area. Why would I need to know all this?"

After three months—with three months left on his listing agreement—he called again, requesting a release of the contract. He didn't want to work with us. At this point, I was okay with that. No deal is better than a bad deal. Despite all the effort we'd put in, I knew I wouldn't make this seller happy. It was better to release and move on than to keep wasting additional energy, time, and resources on this guy.

He relisted with another agent I knew, and about two months later, I was working with a buyer who viewed the property, and we submitted an offer. The agent and I went back and forth but couldn't find a negotiating point. We were about $2,000 off. The seller told his agent, "I have no more money. That's the best I can do."

With the negotiations over, I found the buyer another property, wrote an offer, negotiated the contract, and closed thirty days later. About a month after that—two months after we'd submitted the offer to the angry seller—my phone rang, and it was him. He said, "Okay, I'm ready to accept the offer. I had more money to negotiate with. I've been playing hardball, but I'm ready to accept the offer now."

Confused, I asked, "What are you talking about?"

"The offer we're negotiating. I'm ready to accept it. I'll tell my agent, but I wanted you to know first so you could let the buyer know."

I don't remember how the conversation ended. But I remember that the house sat on the market for another nine months, with at least one other agent involved. It sold for much less than my buyer's offer or the previous offers we'd received.

If we'd stayed with him and fought for the listing, it would have been a painful year, and no amount of return on investment would have been worth that.

12

WORKING WITH UNDER-CONTRACT SELLERS

I t finally happened. Whether on the market for a few days or months, your listing is finally under contract. Now, the income maintenance phase is in top gear. Mythical, magical money at its grandest. I'll teach you how to bring that contract to closing in this section.

Let's go back to 2013 for a minute. Tara and I had begun to work *on* our business more than *in* our business as our team grew. Tara focused on driving sales, and I looked at the bottom line and where we might be losing income.

In reviewing our profit and loss statement from the previous year, I noticed that a column titled *Seller Repairs* had a much higher number than I would have thought—much higher. When I dug in and looked at the detailed transactions that contributed to this line item, I connected previous sellers with their repair items, lawn care, property maintenance, etc. Curiosity took me a step further, and I looked at seller commissions that had been reduced, then connected the repair transactions and the contracts. It was shocking to learn that we'd made small compromises to make the transaction work for a year, which cost us just over $106,000. We'd created a culture where repairs and commission cuts happened without asking if we needed to do so to keep the transaction together. We'd created a culture of paying for the business.

I knew there had to be a more profitable way to do business without losing clients or busting contracts. We were reaching $700,000 in commission at an average sales price of $190,000 (with eighty-nine listings sold in 2012). We paid an average of $1,191 for every listing to close it. That was not good business. We were losing so slowly that we thought we were winning.

To change the culture without losing clients, we first had to learn to keep the client happy (positive) throughout the contract-to-close process regardless of outcomes. Second, regarding low appraisals and inspection results/requests, we needed empathy with our clients, not sympathy. Or, to put it bluntly, we had to stop making the sellers' problems our problems.

> We were losing so slowly that we thought we were winning.

If your friend was in a boat and it was sinking, sympathy would be getting in the boat with them while it sank, offering no other help than to go down with them. Empathy says, "Hey, I know this sucks. Your boat is sinking. Grab my hand, and let me help you out of the boat."

Your clients' problems are not your problems. Your role in the transaction is to assist them in solving those problems, not to pay to repair the home they lived in. You didn't create the storm that damaged their roof. You didn't neglect essential home maintenance over the years that caused mechanical issues for the HVAC. But you can help by walking them through the steps to repair those items.

Next, we learned to connect the sellers to their goals we discovered during the listing appointment. You cannot control appraisers. They offer their opinion of value to the bank. Most appraisers aren't concerned with you or your seller's opinion of the home value. Contrary to what many think, an appraiser doesn't work for the buyer. The appraiser works for the bank, although the buyer pays for the appraisal. The bank hires an appraiser to see if the house is worth the money they've been asked to loan for a property. When an appraisal comes in low, check the appraisal. Are there indeed better comps? Did the appraiser miss something of value in the home? We will have more on this in just a bit.

Do the Work

Your work doesn't end when a property goes under contract; the work changes. The property goes from income production to income maintenance. In other words, you must maintain the contract to earn the income at closing.

Communication must be systematized/automated at this point in the transaction so you keep the seller up to date every step of the way. We do this through our CRM. It would help if you communicated essential dates they need to know, such as:

- Any inspection periods, such as beginning and end dates
- What inspections will take place
  - If additional inspections are in order, when and why
- Lender deadlines for the buying party
  - Pre-approval

- o   Final underwriting and clear to close
- Appraisal and mortgage surveys
- Any final or additional walk-throughs
- Closing date

When communicating the closing date, tell the seller when they need to be out of the property. It's rare, but some sellers don't know they must be out at closing. We've also had sellers rent back the property for an additional time, and we've negotiated early occupancy for our buyers. All must agree to the date to vacate.

Our CRM allows us to enter the dates for specific activities and autogenerates a scripted email with each of the timelines. The inspection dates are emailed, followed by a phone call. Don't rely on the email to do the work for you. If it goes to spam or the seller misses it, the seller will be unhappy when many people show up at their house "unannounced" to look at everything inside and out. Sending an email and making a phone call is a two-punch method; it doesn't matter which happens first.

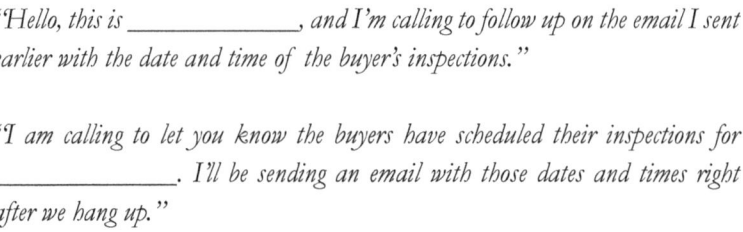

"Hello, this is _____, and I'm calling to follow up on the email I sent earlier with the date and time of the buyer's inspections."

"I am calling to let you know the buyers have scheduled their inspections for _____. I'll be sending an email with those dates and times right after we hang up."

When the inspections are complete, you may receive a request for repairs, even if the property is sold "as-is." This is when you must keep the seller focused on their goals and remind them that selling the house helps meet those goals. Often, sellers will agree to the repairs without argument. In other cases, you may have some pushback or concerns about cost. A couple of scripts that work well for that are:

"The estimate for the repairs comes to about $1,500. Are you willing to repurchase the house from the buyers for $1,500 and start over again to look for a new buyer?"

"I know it may feel like I'm not on your side and that I'm negotiating for the buyer or just trying to get the transaction closed. The truth is, I know you want to sell the house because of _____, and if the buyer walks away from the transaction, the next inspector and the next buyer will more than likely find the same items. When we find the next buyer, they'll most likely request the same repairs. My goal is to help you reach the goal of _____ sooner than later."

"I have a group of reasonably priced contractors who've worked with other sellers. Why don't I help get estimates and take that off your plate? Some of these will allow a 'bill to closing,' so you're not out of pocket now."

Each script works in its own way to reduce the seller's stress by taking them back to their goals or assisting them with what feels overwhelming. Work these scripts into your personality, but don't remove the pivotal pieces that directly engage your client to take action. Too often, agents rewrite scripts in ways that make them less direct. They beat around the bush, typically ending with nobody doing the work. Sellers under contract are typically looking for solid guidance. Regardless of the reason, you'll be the one to blame if the transaction falls apart at the inspection period. So, you might as well direct the seller in the best way possible based on your experience or your mentor's experience. (If you're new, always have a mentor for your first few transactions.)

> Too often, agents rewrite scripts in ways that make them less direct.

Check in with the title company along the way. Never assume that everything is good to go and will be smooth sailing. Allow me to tell on myself here. Recently, we didn't follow up with the title company as we should have, and two days before closing, multiple clouds on the title appeared due to the improper handling of a deed transfer by an attorney. The attorney who did the work "was no longer with the firm." The transaction fell apart, and the buyers couldn't wait the ninety-plus days to fix the title work. Yes, we had the buyer, but I share this story here because it happened to that listing agent. She had no idea—none. This should have been discovered much earlier in the transaction, not two days before closing on a thirty-day closing.

Something else our sellers appreciate is to schedule an early signing, typically the day before the buyers close. Then, on the actual closing day, they can finish moving out of the house without being interrupted to go to the closing. You may have to visit the title company twice, but that's okay if your clients are happier. Besides, it gives you time to connect with the other agent and answer any questions the buyers may have without the buyers and sellers talking, which brings me to my next point.

Never let buyers and sellers talk during the transaction period, especially without you or the other agent involved. It may be tempting or seem like the right thing to do. However, too often, it ends in disaster or an uncomfortable confrontation.

Our team had a contract that fell apart and ended up in mediation over lawn chairs. The buyer said, "Man, these lawn chairs are nice around the pool. I'd love for them to stay." The seller responded, "They are pretty great." In the buyer's mind, that meant the chairs were staying, but in the seller's mind, they're pretty great around this pool and will look just as good around my next pool.

True story. Here are two more examples of sellers talking to the buyers:

"Yeah, that neighbor over there. Huge pervert likes to look over the fence when my wife or daughter are in their swimsuits."

"I didn't mention this in the disclosures, but the dishwasher flooded the house right before we bought it during the last week of construction and made a mess. The builder had to replace a lot of sheetrock. Never had any issues with mold, though." (This was also news to me!)

As agents, our role is to be the voice of our client. When we allow the client to bypass us, we remove ourselves from the equation until something goes wrong. Then, we're the ones at fault for whatever goes wrong. Be your client's voice. Always be a part of the communication between your clients and the other party.

Appraisals

We briefly discussed appraisals earlier in this chapter. Here's a short list of what you need to know. Appraisals are an individual's opinion of value. According to dictionary.com, an opinion is "a view or judgment formed about something, not necessarily based on fact or knowledge." Did you catch that last part, "not necessarily based on fact or knowledge"? Do enough transactions, and you'll argue that an appraisal doesn't match up to facts or knowledge. But here's what you can do to help an appraiser form their professional opinion.

First, give the appraiser the tools they need to be successful, such as the cost of the upgrades, the cost of the pool, the price of the metal building, the remodel cost, etc. During the listing presentation, ask the seller if they have the receipts or can put together an itemized list of the costs of the changes they've made to the home over the years. Help the appraiser justify the cost of the house.

Second, if the property is larger than the tax records indicate, do not rely on your MLS to notify the appraiser or on their measurements. Send the appraiser the new square footage and the source.

Third, send the appraiser the comps you used. Be respectful when you send them. Just let the appraiser know these were the comps you used when figuring the list price and explain why you used these comps. Doing some work for the appraiser up front may go a long way when needed.

If you receive a low opinion of value, the first step is to breathe. Just relax. Getting frustrated or mad at the appraiser won't help. It would be best to be calm in the storm when the seller, buyer, and buyer's agent are all frustrated.

Appraisers don't look at price per square foot like the rest of the real estate community, so when you see an added or subtracted valuation for the price, you'll notice the dollar amount is less than the overall price per square foot. That's because appraisers add value for amenities like bedrooms, baths, garage, pool, storage, etc. So, when an appraisal comes in low, check the house's amenities first. Is all the information correct? Most appraisers won't miss these items, but it's always best to double-check. Sometimes, something as simple as a fireplace can add value.

Next, look at the SQFT noted by the appraiser. Does it match what you have? A few times in my career, a simple closet missed or not counting the SQFT of a staircase up and down can make a difference. Does the floor plan the appraiser has match the actual floor plan? If you find a discrepancy, have a respectful conversation with the appraiser to share your findings. You get more with honey than you do with vinegar.

If you find a discrepancy, have a respectful conversation with the appraiser to share your findings.

If all is correct, then go to the comparable properties. Is there a comparable property that you used but the appraiser didn't? Please share them with the lender and the appraiser. Again, be respectful. When an appraiser changes value beyond a certain amount, the appraiser must explain why their original appraisal was off by so much. That's why appraisers are so reluctant to make changes. So be sure to adequately back your findings and get the lender involved.

Lenders can talk to the appraisers despite what they may say. Many lending companies put the "can't talk to appraisers" policy in place not because it's against the law but because they don't violate rules/laws that state lenders cannot influence appraisers unjustly. However, most appraisal boards will tell you, yes, they can speak to each other, and most times, the mortgage company backs the changes to the appraisal with the appropriate data. Remember that appraisers work for the lender, not the buyer. A suitable lender understands this and will work with you if you can support your findings for a price change. In the end, if it's a reasonable appraisal, it's a good one, regardless of whether it meets the sales price.

If the sales price and the appraisal don't match, you have a couple of options: Either both parties agree to reduce the sales price, you find a negotiated middle ground on price, or the buyer walks from the contract. Even if the seller disagrees, most contracts allow the buyer out of the contract if the appraised value doesn't meet the sales price. Currently, FHA appraisals stick with a property for six months, regardless of the buyer, and VA appraisals stay with the buyer. In other words, VA and conventional loans can potentially be ordered again if sufficient reason is given to the lender or the buyer changes lenders. This is true at the time of this printing, but lending laws often change. Talk to a trusted lender about options if you get a low appraisal.

You now have a basic idea of the process, a few scripts to help you along, and general guidance from contract to close.

The Good

Remember when I said that the seller's problems aren't your problems? This is actually a guiding principle, not a rule. Here's a story about one of our sellers.

She was a sixty-year-old woman with a special needs daughter and was also raising her nephew, and they had to be out of the house at closing. Some minor repairs needed to be made before closing, numerous items needed to be removed that she wasn't taking with her, and the home had to be cleaned. She was at her wit's end but didn't ask for help, although she needed it.

We mobilized our entire real estate team (about twenty people). We showed up with tools, a large trailer, and the motivation to complete everything in a day. Several hours later, the house was cleaned, the minor repairs were done, we had a trailer full of trash, and the seller was thankful.

Unbeknownst to us, the neighbor across the street had spoken to her the day before we showed up. She had conveyed her stress. Time had moved too quickly for her to care for everything, and she was bound. How do I know all this? The day after the closing, the neighbor tagged our team in a Facebook post on his page and the Neighborhood HOA Facebook Group. He couldn't believe what we'd done for her and was singing our praises. Since then, he has reposted that event several times when the Facebook memory pops onto his feed. Thanks to this neighbors praises, we've listed several more homes in that neighborhood.

Sometimes, you must bend the rules and do what needs to be done. But it should always be a conscious decision that's done for the right reasons.

The Bad

There may be times when you get away from yourself. You fight for your client's problems even though you know you shouldn't. Tara and I were driving back from a conference in Texas when an agent called about a listing that was under contract and was nearing the closing date. We had already gone through the repair negotiations portion of the transaction, and now the buyer was asking for the HVAC to be replaced. Tara argued that it didn't need to be replaced per the inspection report. The buyers' agent was insistent. Tara told her that would not happen and asking was ridiculous.

After Tara got off the phone, I was right there with her feelings about the situation. I quickly piped in, "That's ridiculous. Why would she think she could ask for that? We're done with the negotiations. Unbelievable. That's asking the buyer to pay another $8,000 for the repairs he's already done."

Tara and I went back and forth, becoming more indignant. After about twenty minutes, she called the client. She explained what the buyer was asking for without expressing her opinion, and the buyer said, "Okay, that's no problem. I understand."

Tara hung up the phone, looked at me, and said, "What the hell? I know better than to speak on the buyers' behalf."

After a sigh, she called the other agent and told her the seller agreed to replace the HVAC and would sign the addendum with the request.

Though we didn't lose any money in this situation, we did have to eat crow after arguing with the agent without first talking to our client. More importantly, we failed to distance ourselves emotionally, which could have cost us the transaction—all because of our egos.

13

WORKING WITH BUYER LEADS

Regardless of the market, buyer leads have the potential to bring you income in forty-five days or less. You have one goal: to find the buyer their next home. The great thing about working with buyer leads is that when the house is under contract (close or bust), you'll have that buyer forever if you do a great job.

Notice that I said your job is to find the buyer *their next* home. Too often, agents try to find their clients the perfect home, their dream home that meets all their needs. These are impressive goals, but it's also nearly impossible to accomplish. However, when you find out what the client must have, would like to have, and what's on their wish list, you can find the property that most meets your buyer's needs.

I've heard that statistically, only one out of one hundred leads will work with you to close. That's a terrible conversion number and a lot of work for one lead. And yet, I find that many agents use excuses like "They're not good leads," "They're just a bunch of junk," or "I can't get them to set an appointment" to justify why their leads aren't converting to clients.

Perhaps the problem is that the agent and the buyer are working toward two different goals. A lead is when someone inquires about a house. The potential buyer wants to know about the house; the agent wants to tell the buyer how excellent their real estate services are. The potential buyer wants to set an appointment to see the house; the agent wants to qualify the lead to determine if it's worth their time. The buyer is asking questions about the house; the agent is trying to build rapport.

You want to convert a lead to a customer, not just set the appointment. Align your goals with the buyer's goals. Most leads, whether sign calls or internet leads, already know about the house before they call you. They want to set an appointment. They'll ask you if they have a question after you ask them to set an appointment. Don't answer unasked questions at this point.

After you meet them at the house, they will have achieved their first goal, which was why they reached out to you—to see the house. Now, they'll be open to building rapport, learning why they should work with you, and having you show them more houses.

I teach my agents that one out of ten leads will work with you, no matter what. And one won't work with you no matter what you do. The other eight all depend on you. So, if you're converting one out of ten leads, you're only working with people who will work with any agent who answers the phone. If you convert two out of ten, you've only converted one.

You need to figure out how to convert buyer leads to buyer clients and how to keep them as clients until you get them under contract.

Do the Work

When working with leads, it's crucial not to say too much, whether talking about personal stuff to build rapport or real estate. I've heard it said that it doesn't take an intelligent person to make a complicated subject sound complicated; it takes intelligence to simplify a complicated subject. Yes, sometimes you want to impress clients with your knowledge or dazzle them with your bullsh*t. But less is often more regarding how you talk about the market, contracts, offers, etc.

In an essay titled "Simplicity" by William Zinsser, he recounts how President Roosevelt wanted to get his message of simplification across when responding to a government memo that read:

"Such preparations shall be made as will completely obscure all Federal buildings and non-Federal buildings occupied by the Federal government during an air raid for any period of time from visibility by reason of internal or external illumination."

Roosevelt responded, "Tell them that in buildings where they have to keep the work going to put something across the windows."

When the buyer asks how the market is, go beyond "Fantastic." Examples could be:

"Fantastic! Home sales are up 3 percent over last year, but we only see prices increase by 1 percent. So homes are selling, but only a slight increase over last year."

"The local real estate market is sitting at about four months of inventory, which makes it good for sellers and buyers."

"Days on the market are at thirty-five days, so buyers see sellers willing to negotiate a little more than last year."

Notice that each statement includes a statistic followed by an explanation. Of course, I could say ten different things for each statistic, depending on the spin I want to put on it. Be sure not to spin too much. Impress them with more knowledge and less bullsh*t.

When you receive a call, keep it simple:

Buyer: *"I'm looking for a real estate agent to work with."*

Agent: *"Fantastic, I'd love to work with you. Do you already have a property you'd like to view"*

If the buyer says **No:**

Agent: *"Tell me what you're looking for in your next home,"* or

"When are you available to look at homes?" or

"Let's meet at _____."

Notice two things. First, always use the term *next home,* not perfect home, dream home, etc. Those terms set you up to meet an impossible goal, no matter the market. This doesn't mean you won't find a home meeting their dream home status. It just means that the perfect dream home isn't the expectation.

Second, pick up the client in your car and drive them to showings if possible. This is where you can build rapport between properties. Too many agents try to sell a home and build rapport simultaneously. It distracts the buyer from focusing on the home when you're trying to connect with them over your mutual love of golf. When you drive, it allows the client to view the home and fall in love with the home while they're in the home.

Buyer: *"I'm calling about the property at 123 Main Street."*

Agent: *"Do you want to schedule a time to view the property?"*

If the buyer says yes, schedule a time to view the property as soon as possible. The longer you delay, the more time you allow them to change their mind or find another agent to show it to them. Which is why you need to follow up with:

Agent: *"Other than this property, are there other properties you'd like to view? I can save you time and set them all up at once."*

Note: I've even called other agents to say:

"Hello, I apologize; my client called you to set up a showing. I'll be showing them the property at 123 Main St at _____. I apologize for any inconvenience."

If the buyer responds to the original question of "Do you want to set up a time to view the property?" with:

"No, I just want to know _____."

First, answer their questions or let them know you'll get the answers and follow up with them. Say what you will do, then do it. Next, ask these questions:

"Does this home fit what you're looking for?"

"When are you available to look at this or similar homes I may find for you?"

If the buyer says the home doesn't meet their requirements, regardless of its price or size, say:

"Tell me what you're looking for in your next home."

And remember they called because they're looking for a property, not a friend.

You need to have confidence to set the appointment. You don't need to overcomplicate it. Get the address, set a date and time to meet them, and get off the phone.

Sooner is better. And remember, they called because they're looking for a property, not a friend.

Prepare for the Showing

First, never show up empty-handed. The advent of smartphones, iPads, and tablets has made the world a little too digital when providing value. Think of it like this: What do you value more, a digital invitation to an event or receiving a physical invitation in the mail? Yes, you can have all the information about a property from an online portal on your phone; however, I'm from the old school that says when you show up with an actual printed document, you look more prepared than the competition. So, print out the information. This includes a market analysis of the area.

Second, always take a paper contract with you. Again, I know many digital platforms allow you to write a contract electronically and get signatures. Still, a pen and paper can be more reliable than internet services when showing a property. Besides, you must strike while the iron is hot.

I made two big mistakes with one of my first clients. First, when showing them properties, I didn't drive them in my car. Second, I didn't have a paper contract with me. After finding the "perfect home," I asked for the sale; they said yes and began following me back to my office, which was only two miles away. This house was five times our average sales price—not an inexpensive home. I called Tara, who was still at the office. As I told her we were on the way to the office to write a contract, maybe even boasting a little, I watched their car turn onto another street about a half mile from our destination.

I quickly cut the conversation off and called my clients back. They said they "needed to think about it a little more." After sleeping on it the following day, they decided to proceed with the offer. But before we could submit our offer, the seller accepted another offer. It took me two and a half years and many, many, many home tours later to find them their next home. They compared everything after that to the house I lost for them. I say I lost it for them because we would have written it that night if I'd had the paper contract. Even if they'd asked me to wait before submitting it, it would have been ready to go, and I may have beaten out the other offer.

And third, set up at least two more properties to view. If they don't like the first one, you can follow up with:

> *"I went ahead and scheduled us two more similar properties to view in case this house wasn't the one. Do you have time to view these other two homes?"*

Maximize the Showing

Turn on all the lights when you get to the property, but be strategic about it. If you're meeting the buyers at the house, get there early. Lock the door behind you and turn on all the lights. Lock the door so they don't walk in while you're in the back bedrooms. This is for safety as well as for psychological reasons.

If they're riding with you or if you enter the house at the same time, point them to the main living areas and say:

> *"I'll turn on the other lights while you view the kitchen and living room."*

Master bedrooms are private places, and hallways are narrow. No one wants a stranger in their bedroom, so let the clients view it without you. Second, avoid the hallway bottleneck, especially if you show more than one person at a time. Remember, they're there to buy a house, not make new friends. So let them view the home. Stand off to the side and listen to what they say or ask. Then ask:

"Do you love it? Do you want to buy it?"

If you're showing multiple properties, say:

"On a scale of one to ten, how would you rate this home? We'll view the eights, nines, and tens again."

If the property is a no or a seven or less, ask,

"What would make you want to buy?"

Following the no is when you can work to build rapport and ask some follow-up questions such as:

"Are you looking to pay cash for your next home, or are you working with a lender?"

"How much would you like to put down?"

"What monthly payment would work for you?"

"Have you begun the pre-approval process?"

"Is anyone else going to help you decide on your next home?"

"Do you have a house to sell before you buy?"

"What are your goals around buying your next home?"

See Chapter 10 about working with seller leads for what to do if the buyer is also selling.

That last question about their goals is the most critical. When showing properties and writing offers with clients, you want to be able to take it back to their goals, especially during negotiations. You must know their emotional and logical reasons for buying a home. People buy out of emotion and justify their decisions with logic.

Keep Them as a Buyer

Now that you've won the client, you must keep them as a buyer. The key is to always have your next appointment set. Ask:

"When are you available to look at homes again?"

"Are you available tomorrow at _____ or _____ to look at homes? If not, what time works for you?"

If you still need some scripts or things to talk about with buyers, there are two acronyms that I've heard so many times in so many trainings that I couldn't tell you who originally coined them. I just know they work. The two acronyms are LPMAMA and FORD.

LPMAMA

L is for **Location**. Find out everything you can about the area that interests the buyer. A few questions you can ask are:

"What interests you about the location of this home?"

"What areas are you interested in?"

"What moved you to the area?"

P is for **Price**. Find out what's most important to the buyer regarding price, payments, price range, etc. Questions to ask here are:

"What price range do you want to stay within?"

"Would you say you're more payment-conscious or price-conscious?"

M is for **Motivation**. Why are they motivated to buy now? We discussed this in finding a buyer's emotional and logical motivations.

A is for **Appointment**. Always set an appointment.

M is for **Mortgage**. How will they pay for the house?

> *"Will you pay cash for the house or work with a lender?"*
>
> *"Have you spoken to a lender to see the best loan program for you?"*
>
> *"Have you begun the pre-approval process yet?"*

A is for **Agent**. Make sure you're their agent.

> *"Can I assume you haven't found a great agent, other than me, to work with?"*
>
> *"I only work with five active buyers at a time. I just helped someone close on a home, so I'm looking to work with one more buyer. Would you say you're actively looking in the market?"*

What I love most about the LPMAMA acronym is that it works as a guide to finding important information that will assist you in better serving the client.

FORD

The acronym FORD stands for Family, Occupation, Recreation, and Dreams. Like LPMAMMA, the FORD questions help you build rapport with your clients and discover their real estate needs. Be sure that you do not violate Fair Housing Laws when you ask the FORD questions, especially around family. Some of these questions may seem direct, which is often needed to move a conversation forward with a client to discover their potential needs and build rapport.

Family: Before asking family questions, consider what the clients say naturally. If they don't mention kids, don't ask about kids. If they mention kids, then ask about kids.

- Do you have a large family?
- Are you concerned about school districts?
- How long do you think you'll live in the house you buy?
- Do your kids have any hobbies?
- Tell me how you two met.
- What led you to decide to move?

Occupation: Lead from curiosity regarding what your potential clients do for a living. Every job has fascinating aspects, and building excellent rapport is finding out about their passion for their work and letting them share it with you.

- So, what do you do?
- How long have you worked in the _____ industry?
- What led you to a career in _____?
- Do you want or need to be close to your work?
- Does your job ever require you to work from home?

Recreation: Again, lead with curiosity. In my years in sales, I've learned about everything from model trains to open-water diving. I never got into model trains, but one client motivated me to get dive certified, which I now am.

- What do you do for fun?
- Are you more of an indoors person or an outdoors person?
- What's your favorite type of food?
- Are you into any sports?
- Do you have any hobbies?

- Is there a hobby you want to start doing?
- How long have you been into _____?

Dreams

- If you could travel anywhere, where would you go?
- Have you traveled anywhere you would want to go back to?
- If you could do anything, what would you do?
- If you could meet anyone from any time, who would it be?
- What's your dream job?

I could go on for pages with questions, but the questions and scripts aim to give you a place to start building your own list of questions and scripts that fit your personality and style. These questions can jumpstart you when you aren't sure what to say.

Writing a Contract

Remember that price isn't the only negotiable factor when writing a contract. For the most part, every space you fill in on a contract can be a negotiation point, such as:

- Price
- Closing Date
- Earnest money
- Home warranty
- Closing costs
- Loan type

Never assume how a buyer would like to take the title. Ask them:

"How would you like to take the title?"

My recommendation is that you never tell a client what to offer. Guide them, but never tell. Because if you do, if they win or lose, it's your fault. You told them what to offer if they don't get the house. If they get the house and later feel they paid too much, again, you told them what to offer.

Buyer: *"What should I offer?"*

Agent: *"I recommend that you don't offer more than you're willing to spend for the home, but not less. That way, if you don't get it, you know you didn't overpay for it."*

Another great thing to do is call the listing agent to ask:

"How can my buyer win with you?"

This question is aimed both at the listing agent and the seller. Price may not be a deciding factor with a seller. Too often, buyers and buyer agents advise on the quick close to win an offer, and a seller may need more time.

When submitting an offer through email—which I highly suggest versus through an electronic signature portal—be sure to bullet point out the key highlights of the offer. An example would be:

Hello,
Attached is an offer for 123 Main St. The highlights of the offer are as follows:
Sales Price to be $450,000
Closing on May 7th
Earnest money to be $5,000
Seller to leave swingset in back yard
Please let me know if you have any questions.
Regards,
Peter Levinson

First, the goal is to ensure there are no surprises with the seller and ensure you didn't miss anything in the offer. At least once a year, I hear that a buyer's agent forgot to include the closing costs their buyer wanted in the offer, and they ask us what we can do about it. "We" are not doing anything about it! The agent will likely have to reduce their commission to cover their mistake. Don't be that agent.

Second, make sure the seller knows the critical points of the offer so you're not a few days from closing and find out the listing agent forgot to mention (and the sellers missed the part in the offer about) the hot tub staying with the property.

Third, be an agent who's easy to work with. Make it so the other agent can review the offer and copy and paste what you send. Agents who are easy to work with win the most negotiations. I've lost count of the times I've heard, "Your offer wasn't as good as the other, but I told my sellers how easy it is to work with you, which was more important than the price."

Never offer or counter verbally.

Always put everything in writing.

I cannot emphasize these final two things enough. The call I hate the most is when an agent calls me and says:

"Do you think your seller would accept _____?"

My response is always the same:

"I'm not sure. Put it in writing, and I'll submit it."

Even my agents test the "always put in writing" at least once, and it eventually bites them in the butt. Recently, after teaching a class on contracts and emphasizing "No verbals," an agent did just that. A client submitted an offer on their dream home, and the listing agent told my agent, "The sellers have accepted the offer." Before they returned the signed contract, my agent told his buyer, "They accepted the offer."

But before the sellers signed the offer and sent it back to my agent, they got another offer, which the seller accepted. The buyer was justifiably frustrated and no longer wanted to work with my agent, who she felt was untrustworthy. This was a $650,000 buyer.

The Good

When I go to real estate conferences, one breakout session I always go to is the Rookie of the Year panel. It's easy to find a seat because many are open. I guess everyone wants to hear from the big names at the conference, from the agents doing big business. However, I love hearing from agents who have fresh eyes on the real estate business. Most new agents haven't yet been told what doesn't work. When they have an idea, they act on it. Some hit gold, and I hoped to hear how they'd struck it.

One of the panelists said he was a full-time pastor and only had a few hours a week to work real estate. He said he didn't have the luxury of working through a bunch of leads until he found buyers who would work with him. So, whenever he received a lead or a referral, he needed to find a way to make it work. He used social media sites and his database to determine how he was connected to that lead/referral. Once he found that connection, he asked that person to contact the lead as a referral source. Doing this gave him an almost 100 percent conversion rate without spending time calling leads hoping to find a connection. He earned close to $300,000 in commissions the first year using this method. This is from a guy who only works about ten hours a week.

The Bad

I had scheduled ten to twelve houses to show my client and had planned to be with them until late into the evening. At about 3:00 p.m., I came back to the office. Tara looked at me, confused.

"I thought you had showings until late tonight," she said.

"Nope," I said. "I sold them the first house we looked at. Wrote an offer and submitted it."

Now, this sounds like the beginning of a great story. Unfortunately, it wasn't a great transaction. It was rough from contract to close, and they never liked the house after they moved in.

Notice I told Tara, "I sold them…"

This is precisely what I did; I sold the house. I didn't think too much about what they needed or wanted. I thought the first house was pretty great. It was a remodel but a poorly done remodel. Sure, it looked good, but it was lipstick on a pig.

I remember the lesson when I drive by the house with its large red diamond on the three white columns out front. You do not sell houses; houses sell themselves. Our job as agents is to find out what the client needs and show them properties that meet them. When you start selling, you start losing.

14

WORKING WITH BUYERS UNDER CONTRACT

You converted the lead, found them a house, wrote an offer, worked out the negotiations, and now your buyers are under contract. Congratulations! But your work isn't done yet. The buyers have now moved from *income production* to *income maintenance*, meaning that to get that income, you must maintain the contract to closing. Once under contract, you're in the income maintenance phase because you're maintaining the income you produced. This chapter is focused on moving the contract to close.

In terms of being under contract, it amazes me how many agents don't pay attention to the contract they wrote for their client, such as missing dates for inspections or lender requirements. Too often, agents don't even know the contract. Ask yourself, "How many times have I read my contract?" or, "How well do I know the contract?" It's sad when an agent invests so much time, energy, and resources to find a buyer and get them under contract, only to fumble their way to closing.

Hoping or blaming the other agent for any mess-ups or giving the buyer a good closing gift won't make everything okay if you screw this part up.

> In terms of being under contract, it amazes me how many agents don't pay attention to the contract they wrote for their client, such as missing dates for inspections or lender requirements.

The best source for new business comes from the clients you're already working with. When a client is looking for a house, that's their focus. If you do it right, you'll find the most client referrals during the contract-to-close phase. The benefit of having a client under contract is that you're days away from earning the income for your work. And now that the stress of finding a house has passed, the buyer has time to breathe and reflect on how well you've done. A buyer will maintain that joyful emotional state with proactive communication throughout the contract phase. This is the prime opportunity to seek a referral and when they will most likely let others know how great you are.

Don't Lose Sight of the Goal

Here's the catch. Statistically, it's been said that 15 percent of contracts don't make it to closing. When a contract busts, the buyer isn't happy because they've paid inspection and appraisal fees. Depending on when it closes, they could be close to being homeless; in short, their world is in total disarray. This isn't the zone to start receiving referrals unless you're 100 percent on it. Even then, it's not a great zone to be in.

When I first heard the national statistics, I became curious about our brokerage's not-closing rate. I was pleased we were almost half the national average of 8 percent. With twenty to thirty contracts pending, it's easy to say, "next" when a contract busts. The revenue impact isn't too noticeable. But for us, 8 percent was still too high. So, we went back to our systems and processes, looked at where we could better bulletproof our contracts and worked to get that number down to 5 percent. And we've been able to reach and maintain that percentage.

Using our CRM, we automated many touches to the client, lender, title company, and cooperating agent. This all starts the moment the property goes under contract. Each automated touch makes a minimum of one weekly touch call. Reminders are put in place for the agent and closing coordinators for important dates, such as inspection periods.

> When a client is unhappy, the first step is to see if our systems and processes are being followed.

When a client is unhappy, the first step is to see if our systems and processes are being followed. Second, we review the contract to see if we've missed something. Third, we never blame another party. This doesn't make your client feel better. All they remember is the stress of the situation.

Do the Work

It's your responsibility to ensure that all the needed actionable items are coordinated or completed and that your buyer is informed every step of the way. Remember from earlier, the buyer was working off an emotional high of looking for a house, finding it, writing an offer, and contracting it. Now, reality steps in. The emotional high wears off, and it's thirty to forty-five days to close. Many buyers are left with a "What's next?" feeling. It's your role to keep them informed, keep them in contract, and ensure they perform the activities needed to move the transaction from contract to close.

Keep Track of Dates

Just like with a seller, you have specific dates and activities that must take place. Such as:

- Sending a copy of the contract to the lender and title company
- Keeping track of inspection periods, such as beginning and end dates
- Coordinating inspections that need to be ordered, plus any additional inspections requested
- Keeping track of lender deadlines for your client, such as getting them the required documentation
- Paying for the appraisal
- Ordering the appraisal
- Any final or additional walk-throughs
- Closing date

A good CRM has ways to automate many tasks where you input the contract dates, such as inspection times and closing dates. It would help if you also created reminders for yourself, such as a twenty-four-hour reminder about when the inspection period ends, so you can turn in any repair requests to be negotiated.

Too often, buyers either don't think of it or assume that everyone else is performing their duties in the transaction, such as having the lender order the appraisal and paying for it. Never assume. Periodically check in with the lender if the lender doesn't check in with you. We have a standing weekly update we receive from our lenders regarding what's happening or what's still needed with the buyer. If possible, set something like this up with your lender. This way, you won't need to call them for an update, which wastes your time and theirs. You can focus on more income production when you know that you'll receive an update on your buyers from your lender every Tuesday. This also works well with title companies. In the updates, let the lender know if you can help in any way to make things work better. Sometimes, it might take a little push to get the buyer to send what the lender or title requires.

Inspections

Even if the buyer doesn't attend, show up at your inspections. This goes back to a phrase I've often used: It's not a problem until it's a problem. Most items found on an inspection report can be resolved—depending if the seller and buyer are willing to work together to resolve the issue.

What are some everyday items that are found during an inspection in your market that might seem significant to the buyer? In my market, the roofs and foundations frequently need repairs, and there's often evidence of termites. Oklahoma has very clay-rich soil, so foundations tend to shift and need piers. We have high winds and hail, so a roof typically doesn't last beyond its half-life. Furthermore, we average three termite colonies per acre, so we say there are two types of houses in Oklahoma, "those that have had termites and those that will."

Do you see what I did there? I know the major issues and how to explain them so the buyer doesn't think the sky's falling. Learning basic scripts to calm the buyer from the inspection report results is another way to bulletproof a transaction. If you don't know your area's typical, significant issues, call a few inspectors and ask them. A little research goes a long way.

After the home inspector reviews the report with your client, ask if they would like to order additional inspections. Never offer your opinion, such as, "No, I don't think getting a structural engineer is necessary." Unless, of course, you want to be held accountable for any structural issues in the future. Their problems are not your problems; you're there to guide your clients, not to make decisions for them or try to save them money by talking them out of inspections.

If the buyer declines any inspections, always get the denial in writing. It may not seem important now, but you may need it if the HVAC goes out or the roof isn't insurable. If in six months something happens, you have a reference point and can remind your client of the conversation.

> **Agent**: *"At the home inspection, the inspector recommended scoping the ducts, but it was decided not to do that at the time."*
>
> **Buyer**: *"Well, I didn't think it was a big deal then and didn't want to spend the money."*
>
> **Agent**: *"If you like, I can connect you with the company the inspector originally recommended. Would you like me to share that with you?"*

Never point the blame with phrases like, "You didn't want to have the ducts scoped." This will put the client on the defensive.

Repairs and Appraisals

Let's get back to the present. All the requested inspections have occurred, and now it's time to assemble a repair request. Two scripts I find to have the best results are:

> *"Let's put these in order from most important to you to least important."*
>
> *"What are the top three items of importance to you?"*

What may be necessary to you may not necessarily be important to the buyer. This doesn't mean that you won't request every single item to be repaired if the buyer wants to request it.

Be sure to ask for the invoices for any completed repairs. And always be sure to verify the repairs were completed. Never trust that they were done just because they were agreed to. A final walk-through or a reinspect of the requested repair items can save you a lot of future headaches.

If you get a low appraisal, assist the buyer where you can. It may not be your responsibility to fix the appraisal, but if you have a listing agent who's unwilling to help, a seller who isn't willing to lower the price, and a buyer who wants the house, you may have to be the one to do the work.

There's one last item. Send your buyer a list of helpful numbers—a list of utilities or contacts they'll need when moving into the house. It's also a great way to remind your buyer to change their mailing address, ensure the electricity is switched into their name, etc. Nothing's worse than getting a call from the buyer the night of closing, and they're sitting in the dark. Sure, you're technically not to blame, but does that help your clients sitting in their new home in the dark? Who do you think they'll blame?

There's one more thing you might be able to do. After the closing, if your market and the buyer allow it, put a sign in the yard—a small yard sign that says something like "Home Sold" and "Buyer Represented by (your name)." Ask the buyers if you can leave it up for about two weeks. Everyone in the neighborhood already knows who listed the home, but do they know who sold it?

The Good

It was arguably one of my most challenging clients. From contract to close, it seemed like no matter how I communicated with him, I couldn't make him happy. He responded to every update with more questions of frustration and unhappiness. No matter how detailed or proactive my team was, this buyer wasn't satisfied.

Every inch of the contract was scrutinized from when we went under contract to the actual closing. Any misstep by the seller or the agent that contradicted or didn't fulfill even the smallest, most minute detail of the contract was called into question. The seller and his agent had zero wiggle room.

Our routine updates became supercharged. The goal was to anticipate every question the buyer could have before he asked it. Sometimes, we were able to, but he often asked a question or pointed to an accusation we couldn't foresee. I remember thinking, *Who thinks of these things?*

The buyer had already sold his home before contacting us. Usually, in a double close, the client leans toward keeping the contract together. In this case, the buyer seemed like he didn't care if the contract busted. After many phone calls, proactive and reactive, we finally closed the transaction.

For years, when real estate agents sat around and told tales of the most demanding client they had ever worked with, this guy was mine, the most challenging buyer I'd ever had. No matter what my team or I did, he was never happy. Even at closing, I felt the cold wave of disappointment from the buyer. Let's say he didn't make it into our database to follow up with. I didn't think he wanted anything to do with me, and I felt the same about him.

About four years later, I received a call. I looked down at my cell phone, and the caller I.D. showed his name.

"Hello, this is Peter Levinson."

"Hey, Peter. This is _____. You helped me buy a few years back."

I responded, "Of course, I remember you," doing my best not to be sarcastic. "How are you doing?"

"Doing great. I am getting ready to move again, this time out of state. I'd like it if you would sell my house for me. You did such a great job last time."

My jaw dropped, and after the momentary shock of the compliment wore off, I responded, "Absolutely!"

I want to say he was easier to work with the second time, but he wasn't. But because of that first and second transaction, our team improved, even if the client didn't. Count yourself lucky when you get the tough ones. They are the iron-sharpens-iron transactions that make you better.

The Bad

It was a perfect client. Dad was selling because he was elderly. Son was selling to buy a bigger house that would accommodate his family and his dad. They were both selling roughly $180,000 houses and buying $750,000 on up—over a million dollars in volume. There were plenty of opportunities to win more buyers with the two listings, which we did.

There were a few must-have features for their new house, such as two master suites downstairs and preferably a separate entrance for the second master. After many home tours, we finally found the house. It even included a separate third-bay garage. It was the perfect house for them. Both the dad and the son were ecstatic. The dad could have his privacy, and his son and family could have theirs. They were close enough if anything happened, but they had the separation needed to still feel independent.

The contract was smooth. All inspections went well, and the requested repair items were negotiated and completed. Both their homes sold on time before closing. Everything went great. Check one off in the perfect transaction category. Or so I thought.

About sixty days later, I received a call from the buyer, and he wasn't happy.

"The septic tank isn't working properly. It's full. Why wasn't this checked before closing?"

"Let me check the file and verify everything with my transaction coordinator."

I checked the file, and sure enough, getting the septic tank inspected was missed by us and the inspector during the home inspection. It cost an additional fee to do so, and I completely missed bringing it up. The home inspector also missed it during the inspection.

I called him back, "You are 100 percent correct. We missed it and should have spoken to you about having it checked."

"Well, it needs to be pumped, and I'm not paying for it."

"Not a problem. I'll take care of it. It shouldn't fall on you because we should have checked it during the home inspection."

"You better. I can't believe this—unacceptable." With that, he hung up. A perfect transaction switched columns.

It was only about a $450 service, not too much, and we took care of it. Yet, I lost a future client. He was done with our team after that incident. I could make excuses to myself. I could say the buyer was unreasonable in his feelings, or it wasn't technically my fault. Neither of these would solve the problem or change the outcome.

It's not how you start that the client remembers. What they remember is how the transaction ends.

15

WORKING WITH BUYERS WHO ARE SELLING

This chapter will help when you have a client selling *and* buying a property simultaneously. Double-close transactions give you multiple opportunities to create income and win with the client. Of course, you may be reading this and thinking, *That's obvious.*

But did you know that 87 percent of sellers don't use the agent who sold their house when it's time to move?

Double closings and double income also mean you must excel on both fronts. The responsibility isn't just doubled; it is closer to four times the responsibility. You are responsible for ensuring they can get out of one house and into the next on the prescribed dates. You must keep each transaction separate in terms of updates and negotiations while knowing you're the glue that holds it all together while not falling into the trap of "I'm making money on one side, so I'll cut the other side." When you start cutting your commission to make the deal work, it may be a sign that you're missing the mark somewhere.

When you have a seller who has to buy, never assume that they'll use you as their agent to buy. You must treat it as an opportunity to win both sides.

It amazes me when a new buyer's agent on my team asks, "I have a buyer I just wrote an offer for, but they have their house listed with a local agent. Can I do that?" The reasons the owner didn't use the same agent to buy vary, but the top two are 1) The agent is doing a terrible job on the listing side, or 2) Their listing agent never asked them about the buy side. In either case, the agent assumed that listing the house meant they also had the buyer. Never take this for granted.

Working as the listing agent and buyer's agent requires you to act differently. Sellers want to see that you're aggressive in getting their home sold. At the same time, you cannot aggressively sell them a house. You must be relaxed and confident that you can negotiate and ensure that the two transactions close within the time frame your clients need.

> Working as the listing agent and buyer's agent requires you to act differently.

Tara and I have an advantage here when working together. She works with buyers, and I focus on the listing side. We found our personalities were better fitted for each type of client. Or perhaps I should more accurately say that in my early years of real estate, I was better suited for winning listing presentations. You may not have that luxury, and that's okay. Remember not to assume that you're entitled to the buy side of the transaction because you listed a property.

It may surprise you, but some people may not know you can also show them houses to purchase. Or they may be looking at new construction, which you can show and sell. And don't forget For Sale by Owners, to name a few of the "Oh, I didn't knows" I've heard over the years.

We developed a straightforward solution to ensure our clients understand that we'll work together on selling their house and buying their next one. We have them sign a buyer-broker agreement during the listing presentation. If you negotiate your listing commission to keep them as a buyer, check to see if your state laws allow it, and make it part of the listing paperwork.

Of course, the best way to lock them down is to set an appointment to look at houses. It may be a bit before their house sells but know your clients. You don't know what they're looking for if you haven't shown them any potential homes yet. Too often, agents make the mistake of waiting to show houses to their sellers if their house isn't ready to sell or if they think it won't sell anytime soon. The problem is your thinking goes against their thinking. You're thinking of their old home; they're dreaming of their new home. They dream long enough, and they'll find an agent to show them a house.

Do the Work

Doing the work is much like I've outlined in Part 2 about working with buyers and sellers. There are no new processes to convey other than determining if the buy is contingent on the sale. If so, you must double down to adhere to all dates and timelines. Failure of one to close could collapse both transactions or cost the client money to finance the gap between the transactions, such as having to reschedule movers or stay in a short-term rental until the other transaction closes.

I suggest that you keep the sale communication updates and the buy communication updates separate. When working the sell side, keep everything about the sell side. When talking about the buy side, keep everything about the buy side. In emails, update the client on the sell side, then send a separate update to the client on the buy side. This will keep dates from being confused.

If it's all happening during one conversation on the phone, make a clear transition.

Agent: *"Okay, so that's everything on the sale of your house. Now, let's talk about your buy side. Okay?"*

Buyer: *"Yes."*

As silly as it may sound, they need to verbally acknowledge that you're changing topics in the conversation. It helps keep things straight in the client's mind.

It's a little extra work, but you don't want the clients showing up at the home they're purchasing for an inspection at the wrong time while a group of people are at their house for the inspection. Don't let them be confused about what inspections are happening and when.

Sometimes, you have to go slower to go faster. Do a little extra work now rather than a lot later.

The Good

Tara and I worked an open house together on a rare Sunday afternoon. Tara greeted the couple and began a casual conversation. They mentioned they had a house to sell before they could purchase.

"Great," Tara said. "My name is Tara Levinson, and I'll be the agent to sell your house."

Simple, straightforward introduction. Tara and I listed their house, and we sold them a house.

They would have said yes if we'd asked if they were working with another agent. They were working with seven agents to look for homes to purchase. Tara's confidence in selling her home was what won the wife over. Later, the husband got his real estate license and joined our team in 2012, and his wife joined us a few years later. Today, Shaun and Rhonda are top agents for our team.

Before Tara, no other agent had asked if they had a house to sell before they purchased. Tara not only asked rapport-building questions that brought the subject to light, but she also stated she would be the one to do it.

The Bad

"Your agent stole my clients." The call started when an agent called my office and asked to speak to the broker.

"I'm sorry, what?" I responded.

"Your agent stole my clients," she repeated.

I responded with sarcasm, unfortunately. "My agent stole your clients? How did they do that? Did they put them in the trunk and drive off with them?"

"No, of course not. I have their house listed, but they bought it with your agent."

"Did you show them any houses?" I asked.

"Well, not yet. Their house hasn't shown yet."

"Do you have a buyer broker agreement you can send me?"

"No, I haven't done it yet because we haven't looked at houses to buy yet."

"So you listed their house but didn't start helping them buy, so they found an agent who would. Is that what I'm hearing?"

"Well . . . I mean."

"Then I guess my agent didn't steal your clients but helped them find a home to purchase." With that, we ended the conversation.

I probably don't come off as a nice person in this story. It just bugs me when agents act like they own clients. Listing someone's house does not entitle you to the buy side of the transaction. You must earn the opportunity to work with every client. Nothing is a given.

16

WORKING INTERNET LEADS

I heard Chris Gardner speak several years back. He's the businessman Will Smith portrayed in the biographical story *The Pursuit of Happyness*. (Happyness is purposefully spelled that way. If you don't know why, you must read the book or watch the movie.) When Chris spoke, he held out his hand, and his index finger had a bend to it. He said it developed that bend by dialing so many cold-calling numbers daily. Of course, he wasn't dialing a cell phone but an old-fashioned rotary phone. When I heard that, I thought, *Thank goodness for autodialers and the internet.*

The internet lets you cast a wide net into the vast ocean of people to attract many leads. Whether you're working through Google, Facebook, or whatever site you use, each site is available to almost everyone in the United States. You're the fisherman with as big a net as you want to cast out. No boundaries on how many numbers you can dial or how many doors you can knock on in a day. The internet lets you market your brand, funnel potential clients to your site, and more without personally getting in front of them for the first introduction.

In my opinion, internet leads are the last source of business you want to pursue because these are potential clients whom you don't

> The internet lets you cast a wide net into the vast ocean of people to attract many leads.

know, and they don't know you. This book discusses many other ways to get clients, but internet leads shouldn't be ignored.

While working at the plastic folding table in my early days, I first looked for free leads. I came across a little-known site at the time called Zillow.

Leaning back in my chair, I told Tara, "Hey, I'm creating a free profile on this site just in case you get calls or emails from it. It's called Zillow. I have no idea what a Zillow is," I added.

Whether you love or hate Zillow, no one in the real estate industry can deny its influence in the marketplace. Even when internet lead generation was new, industry standards had a meager conversion rate for these online leads, but they were leads we received nonetheless. What I quickly realized was that every lead is a lead. These leads had a valid email address, phone number, or both that could end up in our database.

We eventually started paying for leads from Zillow, but it was after we learned to convert online leads and work our way through

> What I quickly realized was that every lead is a lead.

the ones that weren't sincere. We first learned that these people didn't care who we were or how great we thought we were. They were looking for answers to questions they had about a property. They would have called us if they wanted to talk to us. If we answered their questions and found a way to create value, then the lead was willing to know who we were and about our greatness.

Today, we work with multiple lead sources, have a traditionally high conversion rate based on our systems and processes, and, most importantly, any lead with a valid email, phone number, or both goes into the database. A quick look shows we have over 15,000 leads (with a valid email, phone number, or both), not including specific sites, such as Zillow, that are in our database from the internet. Even at the lowest average conversion of 1 out of 100, the potential is 150 transactions. Take your average commission and multiply that by 150 (for our market, it's about $7,500), and you get $1,125,000. Rest assured, we haven't spent nearly that much to generate those leads, and neither will you. The capital return on investment (ROI) is minimal, so consistently working those leads (using a little elbow grease) will be your most significant investment.

Do the Work

Doing the work with internet leads is just that: work. They don't know you, and you need to get them to. It's said to take seven contacts before a lead will respond. That doesn't mean you have to do the seven. When you reach out to them, they may have contacted other agents six times.

When you make contact, the main thing to do is set the appointment. If they're asking about a house, set an appointment to see it. If they're contacting you about selling their house, set the listing appointment. Rapport building is for when they've seen the house and when you're setting your next appointment.

Too often, agents try to build additional value or rapport on that initial call. That's not what the lead wants. First, give them what they want, which is what they called for.

If you reach out to the internet lead and fail to get a response, don't give up on the first try. By first contact, I mean you've called, texted, and emailed (based on having a phone number or email address). If they contact you through a social media page, and that's all you have, then respond that way. Facebook Messenger allows you to call through its app. If you're not getting a response, try that. What do you have to lose?

After the first day of attempted contacts, keep trying to contact them over the next week or so. We reach out a minimum of ten days. The following are examples of scripts to send to the lead. Take them, use them, and personalize them—or create your own. The main point is don't give up until you've tried to contact the lead at least ten times in ten different ways. I've labeled them text, email, video, and call, but don't let that keep you from mixing them up and using a text as a call or a call as a video.

Text: Hello, this is _____. I just wanted to let you know I'm a real estate agent here in the _____ area. This isn't automated or a robot.

Send a video: "_____ here, just wanted to introduce myself and let you know I'm a real person. Are you still interested in _____?"

Email: I have a list of properties that just came on the market that match what you inquired about. Are you still interested in the same type of properties?"

Call: "Hello, this is _____. I was following up on your inquiry on _____. Will you be looking at paying cash or looking to finance? I ask because I've partnered with a lender who has a few programs that may be able to lower your interest rate for some time. Call me when you're free, and I can give you more details."

Text: Hello, this is _____. Apologies for texting, but I'm following up with someone who inquired on _____. I don't want to keep messaging the wrong person. Is this _____?"

Call: "Hello, this is _____. You registered on my website, _____. I'm following up to see if you found the information on the property you inquired about. I look forward to speaking with you."

Text: Just following up on your inquiry. I wanted to make sure you received the information you were looking for and that aliens didn't intercept you. 👽 😁

Email: Thank you for your inquiry about the property at _____. I can get you to see this property pretty quickly. I need to know what time works for you. Are you available tomorrow at _____ or _____?

Call: "This is _____. Thank you for your inquiry on the property at _____. I can get you to see this property pretty easily. I need to know what time works for you. Are you available tomorrow at _____ or _____?"

Text: This is _____. Thank you for inquiring on the property at _____. I left you a voicemail, but I am following up with a text. I can get you to see this property pretty quickly. I need to know what time works for you. Are you available tomorrow at _____ or _____?"

Video: "(name) here again. Just following up to see if you received the information on the property I sent you. There may be a lease with the option to purchase financing on this or other homes. If this is something you're interested in, let me know."

Text: I received your inquiry on _____. Are you looking for a home for yourself or an investment property? If you are interested in an investment property, I have a few others that may also interest you. Let me know."

Call: "Hello, this is _____. We have a few more properties like this one that will be on the market in the coming months. I'm calling to see what your timeframe is. One of these may fit what you're looking for, and we may be able to get it for you off-market so you don't have to compete with other potential buyers."

Text: *I work with a group of investors who have off-market properties in a private group. Let me know if this interests you. I can add you to my private list and share them with you.*

Email: *I'm not sure if you got my last message, but I have a private list of off-market properties from a group of investors I work with. Let me know if you want me to add you to this private list. Depending on what you're looking for, I can customize what I send you.*

By now, you get the point. Create an ongoing document somewhere with a list of these and your scripts. Add to it every time you come across or create a new one. When you're working to get someone to contact you, then all you have to do is pull up your document and pick which one to use.

And remember, most of all, don't give up or feel like you're bothering someone. After all, you may be bothering someone. The goal isn't to be ignored but to get a response. Most agents give up after two or three attempts to contact someone. Hold out your empty hand, palm up. What's in it? Nothing, right? It's an empty hand. Nothing can be taken from it because nothing is in it. So, keep on reaching out to the lead. They can't take anything from you that you don't have. You only have something to gain, and that's a new client.

The Good – The Bad

There is no story here; I just want to share additional thoughts on leads. Think about a time you've looked over a vast ocean or body of water. Though you don't see the fish below the surface, you know they're there. Millions of fish are swimming around. That's the way I view our database. It's a vast ocean filled with fish waiting to be reeled in. It just takes patience and persistence.

When an agent on our team says, "I need more leads," we give them access to that ocean of 15,000+ internet leads. Each of these leads was already reached out to at some time, but many of them have not bought or sold with us. Many haven't responded. These contacts are swimming around in the ocean of our database.

I combined this as both the good and the bad because much good has come from those leads. On more occasions than I can count, a lead who's been in our database for years responds to an agent and is ready to buy. I remember when a brand-new agent converted a lead who bought an $850,000 home (three times our market average sales price).

I also label this as bad because we're supposed to reach out to every valid lead that comes to us within two minutes. If there's no response after phone calls, texts, and emails, it goes into ten days of constant contact (10 Days of Pain). After that, the agent can move that lead to the ocean as a nurture or mark it as unresponsive. Suppose the lead gets assigned to another agent. In that case, no one has successfully kept up with that lead other than our standard general systems and processes to maintain contact with our database. In other words, the lead isn't getting specific communication to them.

When a lead in this ocean converts, I both celebrate and mourn. I'm excited that the lead converted, but I wonder why the original agent couldn't convert it. I could celebrate, but every lead converted is an opportunity to learn what converted that lead, what was said, how it was said, what was the reason the lead converted, and what we can learn from it.

17

WORKING REFERRALS / PAID LEADS

Referral leads are those that you pay for after the transaction closes. These leads tend to have a much higher conversion rate because the lead comes from a valid referral source. I break these types of leads into three basic categories.

The first type of lead is when you receive a direct referral from *another agent*. With this direct connection and a perfect introduction, you should have a 100 percent conversion as long as you do what you're supposed to in terms of excellent customer service.

The second type is direct leads that you pay for because *a company* refers the lead to you. These companies have websites, and people spend a lot of marketing dollars to drive traffic to them nationally. In return, when the lead closes, you pay them anywhere from 25 percent to 35 percent. An example of this type of company is Dave Ramsey's ELP program.

A third type of lead is a referral from *a relocation company*. Relocation companies connect with businesses whose employees are transferred to another location in the company. Businesses hire referring companies to give benefits to their employee. I will be honest; I have no idea how either company compensates each other, but I know some of the referral fees can be up to 42 to 45 percent of the earned commission.

If you work with these companies, be prepared to know that relocation companies "own" these clients, and there's no getting around them. Suppose they refer to the buy side and are selling. In that case, it's common practice that the referral agreement will require you to pay them on both transactions, whether that was in the original communication or it's something you discovered on your own. If you try to sneak it by, your brokerage will hear about it and can potentially lose the opportunity to work with them again.

In the beginning, we worked with a lot of different relocation companies. Yes, they had high fees, but the positives are that we got loyal clients and an excellent source to build our database with great clients. Relocation companies were our second source of clients at first.

However, it became apparent that in terms of profitability, it was best to avoid relying on these leads from companies that charged higher referral fees, especially since agent referrals or referrals from other companies only asked for 25 percent. So, in 2009, we started our transition away from relocation businesses but kept our focus on developing a network of agents throughout the country for referrals.

> The primary benefit of working with referral leads is the high conversion rate.

The primary benefit of working with referral leads is the high conversion rate. Yes, you're paying for that higher conversion rate, but look at the benefit of the time saved for a faster conversion. Instead of the standard cold call conversion, someone introduced you. We quickly learned to harness the power of leads to grow our business, and we added everyone to our database and worked with the leads to create more business. Once we had the client's information, we worked that lead to make them more our client than the party who referred them.

Working referrals and paid leads are a small portion of our business today. We still work with them and continue to use them to grow our business. They can help us create income as long as we have a strategy for them to be *a portion* of our business, and we're not reliant on them to continue the business.

Do the Work

1. **Contact the lead immediately** and keep doing so until you make personal contact. Just because you received a lead from a referral company or another agent doesn't mean they'll be working with you. If you lose a client, it's compounded when it involves a referral because the referring agent will also lose the referral fee they expected when they entrusted you with the lead.

2. **Regularly keep in touch.** Never assume the client is committed to working with you. Never assume anything. I cannot stress this enough. Buyers are always looking, and sellers may continue to interview agents. Until you get the client under contract for a purchase or get the listing agreement signed, keep setting appointments and following up.

3. **Give updates** to the referring party. Relocation companies will require it. In terms of a referring agent, it's greatly appreciated. When another agent is involved, they are your ally versus someone working against you. Different states do things differently. Sometimes, this produces angst with the referring agent if you don't know the differences between your state and theirs. Keep them in the loop with updates so you can be proactive versus reactive.

   Relocation companies usually have forms you have to complete regularly. For listings, most require a BMA (broker market analysis). This is typically about a three- to four-page document where you evaluate the property and comparable properties and describe your sales and marketing strategy to sell it. Biweekly updates are usually a minor version of the initial BMA. It isn't uncommon for various relocation companies to require additional BMAs every month or two while the property is on the market.

   Companies that refer clients for a referral fee often require updates, too. They're typically not as formal as what relocation companies require, but that could change as more companies seek to increase profit margins by closing more sales.

   You may have to pay two referral fees if the buyer has a family member or friend who's also moving. It's not uncommon for a parent to move with their kids to a new city, and once the company learns this, they may expect a referral fee on that transaction as well. I once heard it said, "Don't step over dollars to pick up nickels." Yes, you may make 25 percent more of the commission in the short term, but in the long term, you've burned a referral source.

4. **Never attempt to hide the transaction**. If you receive a referral and time passes or the thought arises that the referring

person/company may have lost track of the fact that they gave it to you, quickly run from the temptation. Always be ethical. Honor the source of the business. Furthermore, calling someone months later to let them know you've contracted the referred client can do much more for your business. It shows you can be trusted.

Two lines can be drawn—one in the sand and one in concrete. The line in the sand is the one you may move. It may not be wise to move it, but it's movable nonetheless. The line in concrete should never be crossed and can't be moved. Attempting to hide a transaction from a referring source is a line in the concrete. Pay the referral fee and keep your integrity.

Make the referring source your client in the future. Work to develop the relationship with the client so they come back to you in the future, not to the third party who referred them. Of course,

> Attempting to hide a transaction from a referring source is a line in the concrete. Pay the referral fee and keep your integrity.

there will be times when this can't be avoided due to the relationship between the referring party and the client. Yes, you'll pay a referral fee up front, but any future business should come straight to you. Keep up with them just as you would any other client.

The Good

How would you like to travel to real estate conferences for free? Okay, not exactly free, but have the trip pay for itself. Referrals are a way to do just that. I will be honest with you: I should have connected those dots better at my first conference. Sure, I met a lot of agents at that first conference—lots of handshakes, business cards, and promises to share referrals. But when I got home, those cards sat on my desk, then I moved them to my drawer and eventually to the trash.

That cycle may or may not have repeated for several more conferences until I had an enlightened conversation with another agent from our brokerage. Tara and I were riding up in the elevator one evening after the conference when the agent said, "Looks like I already have this conference paid for."

"Really? How's that?" I asked.

"Just received a referral from someone I met here at the conference." He was holding a stack of business cards.

"Good for you," I said. "You found the diamond in the rough."

"Oh, I always get a referral from every conference I attend," he said. "Not usually while I'm at the conference, but someone always sends me one afterward. At every conference I've been to, I've received a referral. You have to keep up with the agents."

At that moment, the cards in my pocket that would usually be destined for the trash felt much more valuable. Lesson learned.

When I teach about customer service, I ask my agents, "Who are your most recurring clients?" The answer is "Other agents." You will deal more with other agents than the buying and selling clients you serve. Now, I add all the agents who aren't in my local area to my database and create a campaign to maintain those connections, so when they think of real estate in Oklahoma, they think of me.

The Bad

Unfortunately, in real estate, referral fees don't need to be disclosed to clients. I say unfortunately for two reasons. First, concerning listings, you and the client aren't negotiating on the same level. They're negotiating the sales price times a percent. For example, if you say you list at 7 percent in an attempt to cover a portion of the referral fee, the seller doesn't know that. The seller thinks you'll get the sales price times 7 percent, but you know you'll get 7 percent minus the referral fee.

The second reason is this: Many online sites and referral companies market to buyers or sellers with bold statements such as "Connect with the Top Agent in Your Area" or "Connect with a Local Expert." But it often isn't the top agent or a local expert. It's someone who signed up to receive referrals, or it's a brokerage that negotiated to receive the leads. Again, the client is in the dark about what's happening on the back side of the transaction, and they may not be getting the professionalism or experience they expect.

We've worked with all types of referral sources that request a referral fee for connecting with a lead. I prefer to pay once the lead closes rather than pay upfront for leads. I want to lead with revenue as often as possible, which means I make the money before paying for the business. That being said, know that you're shaking hands with the devil. I recommend you move your business away from these types of companies as quickly as possible because they stand between you and your client in the relationship.

PART 3

KEEP IT PROFESSIONAL

18

ALWAYS BE PROFESSIONAL

Sales is one of the noblest professions there is. You can have the best product in the world, but it goes nowhere if no one sells it. Even Thomas Edison admitted that Nicolai Tesla was more intelligent than him, but Tesla worked for Edison. Edison knew how to run a business and sell.

In the book *The E Myth Revisited*, author Michael Gerber describes the three hats a business owner must wear: worker, manager, and entrepreneur. You may work for a brokerage, but you are not your broker's employee. You are your own employee. You are the manager and must also be the entrepreneur to grow your business. This means that after you earn your real estate license, you become a business owner, and it's time to act like one and get professional. Many real estate agents don't have a professional business background; hence, they conduct themselves as if real estate is a hobby rather than a professional career.

I don't know anyone who would hire a person to conduct a half-million-dollar business transaction who showed up late, in workout clothes, and said it was their hobby. I want to challenge you to raise the bar for yourself and your fellow agents. Learn to dress the part, act the part, and never deviate. Always be professional, always.

Yes, that also means with family and friends—especially with family and friends. You're a business owner, and you're working when clients are with you.

> Many real estate agents don't have a professional business background; hence, they conduct themselves as if real estate is a hobby rather than a professional career.

Earlier in the book, I mentioned that when friends and family don't work with you, it's because they don't think of you when they think of real estate. Or maybe they did think of you and thought, *Nope*. Harsh, I know. But ask yourself, do they view what you do as a career or something you do? Do they see you as a professional or as just getting by?

Running your business as a professional means knowing how to dress for the client and how to conduct and carry yourself in a professional real estate environment. Conducting yourself in this manner will move your real estate career forward, and it will do wonders for your self-confidence. But it has to be the complete package.

In an earlier chapter, I mentioned the agent who showed up in a yoga outfit for a "Listor Show" (where the listing agent is at the showing, most often at the Sellers request). You might still be thinking, *Who cares? Those weren't her clients*. Wrong. You want to treat every agent like a client because you might do business with them again. Treat everyone as a potential client. Also, do you think that's what her Sellers were expecting when they requested her to be at every showing? I highly doubt it. The Sellers expected her to show up with her A game to get their home sold.

Keep in mind, you never want to come between an agent and their client. Let other agents do it to themselves. One way I can tell that a market is shifting from a seller's market to a buyer's market is when, at a listing appointment, a seller says, "My (fill in the blank: cousin, brother, nephew) is a real estate agent, but I need someone who will get this house sold." In a seller's market, when *anyone* can sell a house, a seller will work with just about *anyone*. But when the market shifts, the real estate clowns get pushed aside for the professionals. They may know you're in real estate, but if you lack professionalism, they won't consider you when they have a crucial real estate need.

The ah-ha moment was in my first ninety days of real estate. I was sitting in my office when an agent walked by and said, "Nice suit. Have a closing today?" He didn't stop to hear my answer. It was more of a statement than a question, and he kept walking down the hall.

I looked at the empty hall, down at my suit, and back at the empty hall and thought, *Was that a drive-by shooting?* I felt wounded. *Is that the perception of me, the industry as a whole, or both?* I took some responsibility for my daily wardrobe but realized it's an industry issue. If you're not on *Selling Sunset*, why dress professionally?

It's a common joke that real estate agents are always late. Seriously, why is that standard practice amongst agents? The excuse is that the last appointment put you off schedule, but sadly, you can win a listing appointment just by saying, "Our appointment is at 4:00 p.m., and it's 3:55." I won a competitive listing simply by showing up on time because the other agent was late.

I can get a leg up on most agents in my market by being viewed as a professional. I professionally run my business and myself and expect professionalism from my team. And this extends to social media as well. That took me a little bit to figure out, but in all fairness, I'm old enough to remember being chastised by my daughter when I asked her what Facebook was.

"It's for college kids, Dad, not for you," she replied.

I dress professionally every day. If it's too hot to wear a suit (it was 108 degrees in Oklahoma yesterday), I find something that works. The best compliments I've received were when wearing golf pants and a polo shirt—and I have a few that stand out correctly.

> I professionally run my business and myself, and I expect professionalism from my team.

It's not only about how you dress. It also extends to how you use the phone, send emails and texts, how you treat other agents, and whether you know the contracts and laws. All that plus more are part of being professional. Let's look at the basic etiquette you should demonstrate in your business.

Do the Work

Identify Yourself

I dialed the number and heard a quick, "Hello?"

Hesitantly, I responded, not knowing if I'd dialed the wrong number. "Hello, is this John Doe with No Name real estate?"

"Yes, it is," John responded with a tone that would keep a telemarketer at bay.

"This is Peter Levinson with the Levinson Real Estate Team, I was calling about. . ."

If you called a business, say a law or doctor's office, how confident would you be you'd reached the correct number if they answered the phone with just a "Hello?" without identifying themselves?

Now, put a potential client in that situation. A buyer calls to ask about a property or for you to come list their house, and you answer the phone with just a "Hello." Your first interaction with a potential client made them feel uncomfortable, causing them to question if they'd dialed the right number.

Now switch it up with a simple, "Hello, this is First Name, Last Name." The caller immediately knows they reached the correct person. I also introduce myself and who I am within that first dialogue. Another scenario that plays out too often is this:

Me: *"Hello, this is Peter Levinson."*

Caller: *"I'm calling about 123 Main Street."*

Me: *"Yes, would you like to schedule a time to see it?"*

Caller: *"Not yet. I have a question. Is there an HOA?"*

Me: *"No, no HOA in that addition."*

Caller: *"Okay, great. I have a client who wants to see it. I'll see when they're available."*

That's an agent calling another agent without introducing themselves. I've had five-to-ten-minute conversations with agents and thought it was a potential client the whole time. How much more professional and respectful to say . . .

Me: *"Hello, this is Peter Levinson."*

Caller: *"Hello, this is First and Last Name with Good Brokerage. I have a client who may be interested in 123 Main Street. Is there an HOA in that addition?"*

Texts and Emails

The same can be applied to text messages. Always introduce yourself in the text. Let the agent know who you are before you tell them why you're texting. It's professional and common courtesy. If an agent thinks they're communicating with a potential client and then, after texting back and forth, they find out you're an agent, that's a letdown and may build some animosity. That's not what you're looking for in a cross-sale agent.

It's sad that I even need to mention the common professional courtesy of introducing yourself to another agent, but you'd be surprised how often agents don't do this. It's an easy practice and sets you apart as a professional.

Let's talk email for a moment. First, always have your business contact information in the signature line of your email. This makes it easy for clients and agents to access it readily: name, email, phone number, and brokerage. Yes, you just sent them an email, so of course, they have your email address, but it simplifies things if they can copy and paste it from your signature line.

Second, though email can sometimes be used like text messaging for sending quick responses back and forth, initial emails should be written using proper sentences and grammar. Even though I put myself in the "writer" category, I can say without a doubt that my grammar is a weakness. So, I must spend more time composing initial emails to agents or clients. Once the relationship is built, quick emails can fly.

Your Wardrobe

I'm not calling for three-piece suits or three-inch heels, but how you dress needs to fit your professional persona. I know agents who are always dressed to the nines and agents who wear T-shirts and jeans, and both are very successful. But I want to point out that you'll attract the clients who are attracted to your style. My recommendation is simple. I advise you to dress one step above expectations. If you overdress, the client may feel a little uncomfortable, but if you underdress, they may be underwhelmed by your professionalism.

Getting dressed is also about mindset. What puts you in the mindset to get work done? For me, t-shirts and jeans don't give me the ready-for-battle feeling. I like a great suit, polished shoes, etc. It makes me feel ready to go, to make calls, and to win clients.

How about you? What makes you feel confident? What takes you from "off of work" to "ready to get work done"? What, when you wear it, changes your physiology? You know what I'm talking about. What can you wear that makes you walk, talk, and act with confidence? Figure that out, and you'll know how to dress for the battle you want to win daily.

Setting Appointments

I've discussed setting appointments multiple times in this book regarding *how* your business moves forward. But I want to mention that setting appointments is also about being on time, respecting the client's time, and being organized. I am a digital planner person. I use the calendar on my phone because it syncs to all my devices. It works great for me. I can put in drive times, reminders to leave on time, etc. It keeps me on track, so I'm always on time and don't overlap appointments.

My wife Tara is a paper planner. She says it allows her to better see her days, weeks, months, and year. She tried to go digital and hated it. She was less organized with the digital approach and went back to paper. So, she always has her planner with her.

There is no perfect planner. The best planner is the one you will use. Whatever you choose, be consistent with it. Professionals respect the time of others and organize their time wisely to achieve great results.

The Good

Thank you for crying, former listing agent. I was initially going to categorize this story in The Bad, but the truth is that it was good for me, even if it was terrible for someone else. It was a million-dollar listing for which a member of our team ended up finding a buyer.

It all started when I received a call from a seller whose property had been on the market for six months. The listing agreement was about to expire. A previous client of mine who lived in the addition recommended me to the seller. As I prepped for the listing appointment, I noticed that the agent who listed the property was pretty well-known in the area, did lots of farming, and even had a billboard nearby that advertised her as the area expert. Upon review of the marketing, I noticed that the photos were great, the description was fantastic, and the video marketing was on point. From what I could tell, everything looked great, but the property still hadn't sold.

When I see this, it typically means one of two things. One, the property is priced too high for the market—not necessarily overpriced by comps but priced over what someone is willing to pay for the property. Or two, the agent didn't know how to work feedback, negotiate, or work for an offer. These things can only be discovered by asking the expired seller questions like:

Can you tell me about the feedback you received?

How was the communication between you and the agent?

How often did you receive updates on your house?

The agent responded by letting the seller know the negative feedback and why the potential buyer didn't want to make an offer. I asked, "How did she overcome those objections with the agent or buyer?"

"I have no idea," he said. "She obviously didn't because we didn't get an offer, not even a low offer." He said, "When I told her I needed a more aggressive agent to sell my house, she started crying."

"She cried?" I asked, a little shocked.

"Yes. She started crying and said she was so disappointed that she hadn't sold it. I felt that was super unprofessional. I understand being upset if you don't do something, but don't cry on me. I asked for a more aggressive agent, which could have been her. Instead of saying she'd be more aggressive, she started crying."

I didn't comment on the previous agent's tears. I just launched into how we work feedback, overcome objections, and press to get offers. Such as:

Based on what you're saying, if the seller does _____, would your buyer buy the home? Would you see if you can put that in the offer? And I'll talk to the seller.

The agent could have kept that listing, but her emotional outburst lost it for her. Our professional response won us the opportunity.

The Bad

There's a line in building a rapport as an agent that you need to find and never cross with each client. Your objective is to help the client buy, sell, or both. When a client shares too much, you may lose that client. I once had a pastor tell me he doesn't counsel anyone in his church. He refers them to another pastor, and that pastor refers his congregants to him. He said, "The reason is, when they share super dark secrets and confess their deepest sins, you now know their shame. And yes, I might help them through it; I might save their marriage. But as they sit in a worship service and listen to a sermon, they think I'm looking at them and thinking of their shame. They think that every message that may touch on what they shared means I'm preaching about them, and they leave our church for another."

It's the same in real estate. I remember the first time I was showing clients properties, and the couple started sharing things about their relationship that had me thinking, *Why are they telling me this?* I did my best to play it casual and professional and steer the conversation in another direction, mainly because it was awkward. The clients didn't seem to mind; they were laughing and carrying on like it was no big deal, as if we were all close friends hanging out.

After dropping them off after viewing properties, we set up a time to go out again. They ended up canceling through text later that night, and I never heard from them again. They disappeared into the infinite nothingness.

Lesson learned. Yes, sometimes clients go into inappropriate conversations on their own. They share embarrassing stories or tell you personal things about their lives. The best way to quash that is the most direct way.

An agent on my team had a client who also thought his job was to be her counselor. He finally had to tell her, "I'm here to find you a home. I'm good at that. But I'm not a counselor." She didn't get upset and respected that he was upfront with her. I'll take it back to what you do for a living: You sell real estate. Stick to that.

19

RESPECT THE AGENT

I've mentioned several times that your number one client as a real estate agent is other agents. You'll likely work more with another agent than you ever will with an individual client. Agents are your gateway to showing properties, getting offers accepted, and working through transactions. Furthermore, they may help you stay out of trouble if you accidentally do the wrong thing.

Your goal of respecting the other agent is to benefit the client and your career. Wouldn't you like to submit an offer in a multiple offer situation and hear the other agent say, "Your offer wasn't the best, but I told my seller that you're easy to work with, very professional, and do your best to make the transaction work."

I've heard this so often that respecting other agents is worth it, especially when I've had to back my ego out of a situation to benefit my client rather than satiate my need to be right or justified. As I've told other agents countless times in my career, "You can have ego, or you can have money, but you seldom can have both." Trust me, the respect you pay other agents will go a long way.

Too often, I see agents treat other agents as adversaries, even when working together on a transaction. Yes, they are the competition. But like a good UFC fight, respectful fighters hug it out afterward, even when one is all lumpy and covered in blood. You can take care of your client, negotiate with a "never split the difference" person, and still have a professional working relationship with other agents.

> "You can have ego, or you can have money, but you seldom can have both."

What do you gain by making another agent feel small? You may feel better about yourself and have a small moment of victory. But in the long run, you'll have the reputation of being an agent who's challenging to work with.

I'll admit that I've advised clients to avoid offers from difficult agents. "Yes, the offer is better," I might say. "But in the long run, you may wish you hadn't accepted it." It's still the seller's decision, but if and when the transaction goes sideways because of the other agent's business practices and how they conduct themselves, I know I've warned my client.

The Levinson Real Estate Team has been number one in our market for years. And I believe a contributing factor is that we don't act like it in terms of our egos. I remember the first time Tara told me about a conversation she had with a new agent. The agent called and said:

Agent: *"Hi, my name is _____. I've been in real estate for about a year, and I was wondering if you had time to meet for lunch. I would love to ask you a few questions."*

Tara: *"Of course, how does Tuesday work?"*

Agent: *"Seriously?"*

Tara: *"Yes."*

Agent: *"Oh my goodness, I thought you would say no, but I had to ask anyway."*

Tara: *"Why would you think that?"*

Agent: *"I mean, you're Tara Levinson."*

Tara: *"Yeah, and you're _____."*

The first growth/leadership book I ever read was when I was a young Marine, written by the then-commandant of the US Marine Corps. I read this line in the book to Tara: "Stars, bars, and chevrons are only indicators of the rank one holds at a particular place in time." The new agent today may be a top producer in a year or so. And just because you're on top today doesn't mean you'll be on top tomorrow. Treat everyone as if they might outrank you one day.

Always work hard to be on top, but don't do so by stepping over others. Be competitive, not ruthless or a bully. Bullying may win the battle, but it will be your undoing over time.

I know I'm respected when an agent calls to tell me that someone on my team "may have done" something that's a violation and then follows up with, "I know you always try to do the right thing." That kind of call allows me to fix the issue. I've also heard individuals at the real estate commission say, "I know you always try to do the right thing." And they do know that. I always try to do the right thing, and that's become my reputation.

Next, I'll share some scripts and ways of communicating with other agents to show you how to win without being a jerk.

Do the Work

Sometimes, going to war and then de-escalating a situation might be tempting. Before going to war, check your ego. Ask yourself what benefits you or your clients will receive if you come out swinging. Let me give you an example from one of my agents who checked his ego and composed a great response to a co-op agent.

Our office had emailed the co-op agent requesting the treatment repair request form. The deadline for her to send it was less than twenty-four hours, and we hadn't received it. She emailed back and said she'd sent it and would not send it again. She said our office "needed to find it because she was on vacation and would not be resending it." She also added a few insults about our team and how we do business. Our agent responded with the following to the co-op agent:

> I appreciate your frustration, as sometimes it can be confusing, so I wanted to clarify. Currently, there are three people involved in this transaction—me (the buyer's realtor), Josh (the transaction coordinator), and Tasha (Operations Manager,) who is Josh's boss and is taking care of things while he (Josh) is out of town.
>
> It's great that we have a team that can keep a transaction going and still allow people the opportunity to have a vacation. I've been CC'd on every email from Josh and Tasha and haven't seen the TRR response from your client. One of the great things about our team's dynamic is that we also have access to everyone's files. Tasha and I cannot locate the TRR received from your client in any of our emails, including Josh's.
>
> I understand you're on vacation, and I think that's great. Is there someone in your office who can assist while you're out? We're happy to talk to them.
>
> Regardless of whether this is a three-person team or a one-person team, sometimes documents get misplaced or lost due to a typo or many other reasons. I understand that you feel you have sent it, but we haven't received it yet and/ or cannot locate it; as such, we request that you resend it, so we can continue this transaction to best serve both of our clients.

The co-op agent was a broker with an entire alphabet of real estate training designations in her signature. Unfortunately, all her designations didn't teach her to respect other agents. And yet, how she reacted and conducted business will never change how we react and conduct business.

That email from our agent should work as a template for you when responding to a combative agent. Notice that the first sentence acknowledges the other agent's feelings. Often, when someone is frustrated, they want to be heard. So let them know you hear them, "I understand your frustration . . ."

Second, he tells her what's happening on our end, praising the team for assisting him in a thankful manner, not condescending or in your face. Other examples could be:

"I appreciate how . . ."

"I can see how someone could be frustrated . . ."

"I can see how it could be frustrating . . ."

The main thing I hear when a transaction goes sideways is, "No one is communicating with me." There usually is communication, but it's not what the co-op agent wants to hear. For example, a lender may say, "Another day, and we should have an answer." You email/text/call the co-op agent to let them know you still don't have clearance to close on a transaction that was supposed to have closed already. After a few days, the agent may say you're not communicating even though you've been touching base daily. The problem is that you can't give an answer you don't have, and the co-op agent wants/needs something more than "any day now."

First, acknowledge the other agent's frustration. They're accountable to their client, and the client wants answers. You may say something like:

"I completely understand your frustration. Your client must be frustrated as well."

Second, remind or ask them about previous conversations:

"I've messaged you almost daily with exactly what I hear from the lender, have I not?"

"You've heard from me, but it's not the answer you were looking for. I understand that can be frustrating. Please understand that we communicate exactly what we know even if it's not the answer we want."

Acknowledging the other agent's frustration takes the wind out of their sails. The goal isn't to be defensive or offensive in your response. Too often, with difficult agents (or clients, for that matter), we want to label them as difficult or crazy. Remember, villains are the heroes of their own story, and what we label as "crazy" is not understanding the other person's point of view. You don't have to buy into their emotions, but empathy goes a long way in keeping a transaction together.

Know the Contract

You may need to educate the other agent about the contract. I speak more about contracts in Chapter 21, but for now, let's look at how to handle a situation where the other agent is difficult because they don't know the contract. This, unfortunately, happens more than it should. You could argue back and forth with an agent, but what I teach my agents to do is the following:

Agent,

According to the contract (insert excerpt from the contract), the (buyer/seller) does not have the right to request a release of contract with earnest money being returned. Since this is a contract issue involving earnest money, I've

CC'd my broker to verify that I'm correct. I recommend getting your broker involved, too.

Sincerely,

Agent

Nine out of ten times, the other broker will teach the co-op agent for you. Don't go to their broker; include yours in the conversation and gently suggest they do the same. This has worked for everything from earnest money disputes to sellers not wanting to transfer deposits on a sale with a tenant in the property.

It's easy to respect the other agents if they're easy to work with. The challenge comes when you're dealing with a not-so-friendly agent. Remember to always be professional and put in the work even when the other agent isn't respecting you. In the end, you'll win and be in the business longer. I could give you a laundry list of agents in my market who were at the top of their game but were challenging to work with—and are no longer near the top. I believe other agents avoid working with them whenever possible.

The Good

I'm the only one who gets to "right fight" in our office. By that, I mean that if an agent outside our office breaks a rule or a law or is doing things the wrong way, my agents know to smile, step out of the situation, and let me take care of it. If you're the broker of your office, you'll have to handle those things, but if you're an agent, that's what your broker or team leader is for.

Just last week, one of my agents called with the following situation. A transaction was a couple of days from closing, and the other agent (the listing agent) was reviewing the settlement statement and noticed it said the seller was paying closing costs. He then looked at the contract, and the contract's finance page that the seller signed showed the seller would pay $2,500 of the buyer's closing costs. The selling agent had missed that. The seller missed it. The listing agent called my agent:

> **Other Agent**: *I missed the part in the contract where the seller pays closing costs.*
>
> **My Agent**: *Oh, okay, it was on the finance page.*
>
> **Other Agent**: *I will have to lower my commission to cover it.*
>
> **My Agent**: *Man, that sucks, but I appreciate you doing that so there aren't any issues. I just checked the email I sent you, and I usually bullet-point the main points of the offer. I noticed I didn't do that this time.*

They exchanged a few more pleasantries, and the conversation ended. About twenty minutes later, the agent called back.

> **Other Agent**: *You know, I thought you didn't bullet point the offer when you emailed it, so you're responsible, too.*
>
> **My Agent**: *How's that? That's not a requirement. We do it to help out. It's still in the contract on the finance page.*
>
> **Other Agent**: *You know, no one reads that. So yeah, you're responsible, too. I spoke to my broker, and she agreed.*
>
> **My Agent**: *You know what? I won't take financial responsibility for this, but please feel free to call my broker or have your broker call.*

He hung up and called me to give me the scoop. I want you to notice that my agent didn't say to the other agent, "You fool. What do you mean no one reads the finance page? Of course, agents are supposed to read it; it's part of the contract. It's your job. It's not my responsibility to read and explain the contract to you so you can explain it to your client." Second, he let the other agent know he wouldn't lower his commission, and if he had any questions about it, he should contact me, his broker.

The transaction closed. The buyer's closing costs were paid. The listing agent covered his mistake by lowering his commission, and I never received a phone call from anyone.

I put this story under "The Good" because of how my agent handled it. He responded without being combative and let the other agent know he could contest the issue with me if he wanted.

Respecting other agents doesn't mean lying down and getting walked over. It means being respectful when they say something as idiotic as, "I didn't read through the contract, so it's your fault."

The Bad

I was walking through Office Depot when my phone rang.

Me: "Hello, this is Peter."

Other Agent: "You said the utilities were on."

Me: "I'm sorry. Who is this?"

Other Agent: "This is _____. We're doing the inspections at _____, and the water isn't on."

Me: "Okay, yes, it's a vacant property. But I checked, and all the utilities are on."

Other Agent: "Well, there's no water."

Me: "Are you sure? The water was on."

Other Agent: "No. There's no water, and you knew we had inspections today. This is ridiculous."

Me: "Okay, can you have the inspector turn it on at the meter for the inspections, and I'll call the water company."

Other Agent: "We can't."

Me: "The inspector won't do it?"

Other Agent: "No. We tried, but there's a giant hole in the street and yard."

Me: *"What do you mean there's a hole?"*

Other Agent: *"There was a note on the door that said a water line burst this morning, and the city is fixing it."*

Me: *"Hold on. You're yelling at me because there's no water because a city water line burst this morning, and the city is fixing it right now?"*

Other Agent: *"Yes. You knew we had inspections today. This is ridiculous. The water should have been on."*

Me: *"Are you stupid?"*

I don't remember much more of what I said after that. I remember losing my temper and saying a few more choice words to the agent. When I hung up, Tara looked at me, shocked and angry.

Tara: *"You can't talk to agents that way."*

Me: *"That agent is stupid. And I bet she's divorced."*

Tara: *"Why would you say she's divorced?"*

Me: *"Because someone's left her."*

Again, I saw the shocked look on my wife's face. I know I didn't say nice things to or about the agent. I've matured and grown since then. Yes, it was an unbelievable but very genuine and authentic conversation. Yes, the agent called to yell at and reprimand me. But her actions should not have dictated my actions or responses. It's my job to be the professional—always.

From that point, Tara took over the transaction. She handled all conversations with the agent. Yep, she fired me from that deal. It makes a funny story now, but my reaction was anything but amused back then.

Coincidently, as I'm writing this part of this book, I was CC'd on an email. The same agent—not with my brokerage—emailed my team, "This is bullsh*t." How did this email come about? A closing coordinator on our team asked her if she'd had a chance to review the repair request form we'd sent. She said she'd sent a response back the day before. Our team member asked what email address she'd sent it to.

The other agent said, "I'm not going to tell you. It's not my responsibility to let you know that." Yes, you read that correctly.

My coordinator then asked, "Did you speak to anyone to let them know you'd sent it?"

Her response was, "No. Why would I do that? That's not my job."

The buyer's agent looked through his email and several other admin emails in case it went to one of their email addresses, and he found nothing.

The coordinator then emailed the agent again and said, "Could you resend the response to this email? We've looked everywhere and don't see we ever received it."

This is what elicited the "This is bullsh*t" response. Ultimately, she finally admitted she'd sent it to the wrong person. I share this story with you so it will live in infamy as the bad way to handle a situation. We should never email a co-op agent with the words, "This is bullsh*t."

20

KNOW THE LAWS

Know the laws. Know the laws. **Know the laws!** I cannot stress this enough. When studying to earn your real estate license, you were taught the laws—what not to do to lose your license or get sued. It's a joke among agents that most real estate schools don't teach you how to sell real estate; they teach you the laws (which is why I wrote this book). But all kidding aside, I can't emphasize enough the importance of knowing the laws. Knowing the laws is knowing the rules of the game. If you know the rules, you know where the boundaries are. And what's more important than knowing what *not* to do is knowing what you *can do* and *how to do it legally*.

Knowing the laws will keep you out of trouble and help you better serve your clients. It's not about being the real estate police for other agents. It's about being the person others come to when they have questions. I can't tell you how often other agents and brokers call me with questions. A local builder I greatly respect lists her properties because she's a broker. She knows I'm available to discuss a question whenever she has a question. She sees me as the local expert. She's more willing to work with us when we bring her offers.

I once heard Tony Robbins say, "I have hundreds of people working for me, and at any time, someone is f*cking something up." He wasn't saying this to be negative but to illustrate that people will make mistakes if you work with people. When brokers know you always try to do the right thing and give them that same courtesy, they'll call you directly if you or someone on your team makes a mistake.

My first real estate broker once asked me a question. He said, "Do you know who gets in the most trouble in real estate?"

Being a new agent, I thought he was making a point. So, I responded, "New agents?"

"Nope. New agents tend to follow the rules they learned in school, know enough to know what they don't know, and are cautious of the rules and regulations. The ones who've been in the business for a while cause the most trouble. They assume they know what they're doing without asking questions, or they've crossed a line so many times they no longer know where the line is."

That conversation stuck with me. I made it a point to learn where the lines were (the rules, regulations, and laws) and to never assume that I know what I think I know. I keep a copy of the Oklahoma Real Estate Rules and Regulations on my laptop and iPad. Even if I know the answer, I go back to the source and double-check myself. If I have a question about something in the law, I contact the Real Estate Commission or a Board member for clarification.

> Even if I think I know the answer, I go back to the source and double-check myself.

In the beginning, this took a lot of my time. But now it's a habit to review any new changes and to review the laws and regulations at least twice a year, in addition to the required training our state mandates.

You may think, *But that's why I have a broker.* That's true. If you're not a broker, you probably have or should have someone in your brokerage to ask when you have questions. I didn't want to wait for that. For example, when it came to marketing, creating a marketing campaign and then waiting to find out if it was legal took too long. Mainly, when I wanted to be first to market with a campaign, I learned the law and created campaigns above board.

Knowing the laws also allows me to handle real estate bullies professionally. When my team or I receive a call from someone threatening us who says we did something wrong, I can ask, "How do you know this?" Then, I can respond to them professionally.

"I understand how you could feel what you're saying is correct. I also can appreciate where you're coming from. Fortunately, I know what the rules and regulations say in this instance and verified it before moving forward. If you like, I can send you the excerpt I reviewed before moving forward."

My agents believe in my ability to lead them down the correct path to ensure that I'm protecting their real estate licenses—which is their key to creating income for themselves and their families. Yes, it is mind-boggling that any agent would risk their license due to a lack of easily obtained knowledge. Don't be that agent. Know the law.

Do the Work

Doing the work regarding real estate law is boring unless you love reading rule books—like if you buy new board games, not for the gameplay but for the opportunity to read new rules. That isn't me. But I make it my practice.

First, download a copy of all the rules, regulations, and laws that govern your state and Board. Now, using your calendar, put yourself back in school. Schedule learning time, blocking when you'll work through each book and how you'll finish it in a specific amount of time. I find most agents fall out of the business because they stop learning. If that's you, then it's time to start learning again. In Oklahoma, November is typically when any new rules or regulations are issued. Find out when your state updates yours and make it a practice to read them.

To keep yourself out of trouble, look for the following red flag statements when an agent or client suggests how to do something:

"Here's how we get around this . . ."

"Who's going to know . . ."

"I've done this before, and it wasn't a problem . . ."

"We can do this outside the contract . . ."

"We can do an addendum outside the brokerage . . ."

Remember, it's not a problem until it's a problem, and anything done "outside" may put you outside.

Attend your state's real estate commission meeting if possible. Here, you can see what other agents did that may have put them on the wrong side of the law. This may seem dark, but it's why I read the book of Job so much in the Bible. I want to learn the lessons he learned from his experience rather than have to learn it from my own experience.

Second, it shows you want to learn to do the right thing. If ever you end up in the hot seat, leniency may be given. This isn't a guarantee—just a good practice that has worked for other agents nationwide.

You know the right thing to do, so do it.

The Good

"Let's see if we can figure this out." A few years ago, I received that response from a regulatory group I'd contacted when I discovered we "may have done something wrong." Both the seller and the buyer were aware of all the activities regarding the contract. The other agent had created the situation, but my agent went along with it since it was "in the contract, so it must be okay."

In this situation, the Oklahoma Real Estate Laws had changed around how wholesale investors could market and sell properties. The listing agent and broker had misunderstood the law and inadvertently involved one of the agents on my team in a violation. Because I was responsible for supervising my agents, I was now accountable. The listing agent assumed that everyone agreed with the law if everything was disclosed. The agents and brokers were accountable for the violations without walking through all the details.

Kudos to the agents for keeping everyone on the up and up, clearly communicating everything with the buyer and seller, and putting everything in writing—even if it was illegal. Since everything had been disclosed to all parties involved, coupled with the fact that the regulatory body knew our reputation for always trying to do the right thing, everyone was saved from any fines or other repercussions when I brought the matter to the Real Estate Commission's attention to find a solution. I know I'm being vague here by giving you just enough details to understand the basics of the situation, but I don't want you to focus on the drama. I want you to remember that the value of having a reputation for doing the right thing and being able to spot when something isn't right is crucial.

In this situation, I spoke with someone to devise a one-time solution to a problem. Interestingly, bringing attention to the matter created a talking point for the following real estate commission meeting.

The agents involved were lucky that it had fallen into a gray area that leaned more toward wrong than right, and the Board could see where better clarification was needed. By being upfront with the problem and confessing our sin, I created value with the powers that be.

I also created value with the other agent. A completely different agent had somehow gotten wind of what was transpiring and filed a complaint against her. When I got involved, the other agent in the transaction had just received notice that the commission was investigating her. When I told her that I had a solution that would clear us all and that the investigation had been halted, she was more than thankful. Once again, more value was created amongst our best clients—other agents. As for my agent, yes, more value was created. Once again, I showed her I could protect her license and help get her out of quicksand.

When running a team or brokerage, a good agent will recognize the value that cannot be quantified with low splits and office fees. They see value as what is made and what is saved. In this situation, I was able to save the transaction and keep her from being fined or worse.

Three birds with one stone—simply by knowing the rules and seeking clarification where clarification was needed.

The Bad

This story takes place before my real estate career but best illustrates what happens when someone fails to follow the rules. When I was an active-duty US Marine, a fellow Marine thought it would be hilarious to change all the numbers on the barracks doors in the middle of the night. I knew who did it because I'd gotten up at 4:30 a.m. to go on a run. I saw him with a screwdriver and a smile as I walked out of my room.

Let's say the sergeant in charge didn't find the humor in it. Later that evening, all hell broke loose because the sergeant wanted to know who'd done it. No one confessed. The whole barracks would be reprimanded if no one confessed because he knew someone knew something.

The sergeant lined up every Marine who lived in the barracks to question us. I approached the culprit and said, "Hey, Marine, I'm going to the end of the line. You know that I know. I believe in giving a Marine a chance to square himself."

When I finally stood before the sergeant, I asked, "Has anyone confessed?"

He said, "No."

"Seriously?" I responded.

Now, I was in a dilemma. I could keep quiet and lie about knowing anything, meaning the entire barracks would be in trouble for one Marine's actions—or I could be a rat. I chose to be the rat.

Why? I gave the man an opportunity to do the right thing. He chose not to take it. He chose to let everyone else suffer because of his choices. He could have come clean hours earlier. Knowing my fellow Marines, even the sergeant who was pissed, he would have been in trouble for the prank, but it would have meant extra latrine duty, not being busted down in rank. He also would have become a legend in the barracks for years.

Also, he lied when he stood before the sergeant and was asked if he did it. He said, "No, it wasn't me." Unfortunately, he chose not to act with integrity. A Marine (or person) who can't be trusted cannot be trusted.

This experience taught me two things. First, when I f*ck up, I need to do the right thing to make it right. If that means confessing, I'll confess. It's never, ever worth lying. That Marine ended up getting busted down in rank—not because of the prank but for telling a lie in front of a formal investigation. That Marine wanted me to give up my integrity to protect him.

Second, always give someone a chance to make it right. This has served me well, and the favor has been returned multiple times. In real estate, it's often not a matter of someone breaking a law; it's a matter of what's the right thing to do.

From my conversations with board or commission members, they don't see it as agents getting in trouble or fining them; they want to protect the public. What better way to protect the public than to help your fellow agent do the right thing?

21

KNOW THE CONTRACTS AND SUPPORTING DOCUMENTS

We spent a whole chapter discussing why you should know the laws, what to teach yourself, and how to learn the laws, i.e., the rules of the real estate game. The next step is to know the pieces of the game. If the laws, rules, and regulations are how you play the game of real estate, then the contracts are the game pieces. For this book, let's call all the contracts, supporting addendums, and such *contracts*.

In real estate, contracts are tools that legally bind a client in a transaction. Without real estate contracts, there's no need for real estate agents. Anyone can open a door and turn on the lights. That's not meant to be facetious. It's true; every day, doors are opened and lights turned on by people who aren't real estate agents. The value of a real estate agent lies in successfully placing a client under contract to buy or sell a property. Without the contract, we are powerless. Knowing the contract makes you a better negotiator, qualifies you to handle opportunities, and helps make your clients more comfortable before, during, and even after a transaction has closed.

> In real estate, contracts are tools that legally bind a client in a transaction.

Take, for example, a buyer-broker agreement—the contract a buyer signs when they commit to working with you. I've had agents say, "They aren't worth the paper they're printed on." I would say, "Yes, that's correct. If that's the value you place on the buyer-broker agreement, that's what it's worth." I suppose an agent would have to sue a former client who signed a buyer-broker agreement but purchased without him. I say *suppose* because I've never heard of an agent doing that.

However, I have found that this particular contract has three significant value points. First, many buyers honor the contract either due to their integrity or because they signed and committed to it. Second, if they contract with another agent, many brokers will give you a 25 percent referral fee if you have a buyer-broker agreement with that client. Third, it takes an agent one step closer to writing a contract with the buyer. If you have the business acumen to get the buyer to sign it within the first three times you show them properties, you're more likely to ask for the sale. You know, "Do you love it? Do you want to buy it?"

You may think, *I don't need to lock someone in like that to get them to work with me. I should do a good enough job that they want to work with me.* I will be as blunt with you as I am with the clients I coach. Are you ready? Here it is: You are a coward. That's why you don't ask a buyer to sign it.

No, Peter, that's not true.

Really? If you didn't have to have a listing agreement to list a property (because it is a real estate law), would you?

Most agents I've posed this question to respond in their defense. *Of course, I would. When you list a house, you invest money and time to do so.*

Then, I stare at them briefly and let their response sink in. And I follow it up with, "So, showing houses is free? It costs you no time or money to show clients houses?" The truth is that many agents would list a house, spend money marketing it, and say, "If I can't sell it, I didn't do my job. And I should market the house so well you want to keep working with me."

Do you see where I'm going with this? This is only one piece of the contract, and understanding how it protects you and commits a buyer makes you a better agent. We haven't even gone into the specifics of the document and what the spirit of it is. You'll have to discover that because it depends on your state's contract requirements.

I use the buyer-broker agreement as a teaching document for all the others because if an agent doesn't offer it, they'll likely hesitate on other parts of the contract. I have a saying around contracts: "There's no such thing as trailing docs." Trailing docs are the supporting addendums to the contract that your broker requires, but you don't have the buyer sign until you have an accepted contract. Then, you email your client and say, "I have some trailing docs 'my Broker requires.'" Coward. Again, you only have these because you're uncomfortable asking buyers to sign the documents.

Agents who ask buyers to sign buyer-broker agreements early in the process write more contracts than agents who don't. And that's why I spent so much time on this one portion of the contract. It's another key to creating more income for yourself in real estate sales.

Do the Work

When was the last time you read through your contract? Top to bottom. Every page. Most agents tell me it's been a while—or never.

Here's your first assignment. Get five highlighters, each a different color. Then, read through the contract once. Highlight anything that jumps out at you—something that makes you say, "Oh, I didn't know it said that." Then, wait a few days and reread it, this time with a different colored highlighter. Repeat a few days later with another highlighter. Do this a total of five times. It never fails. Even on the fifth read, you'll highlight at least one thing.

If you have a question, take it to your broker. If your broker doesn't know the answer, take it to the party that wrote the contract, your MLS, or the real estate commission. I was reading through a vacant land contract and could not understand the jargon for the life of me. When I called the commission, they couldn't answer my questions. So, they gave me the info for the attorney who'd written the contract years earlier. I called him, and we had an excellent forty-five-minute conversation about what the written contract meant and its "spirit." He admitted the section in question wasn't clear, and he said that he and the panel that put it together struggled to document the "spirit" of what they intended.

You may be asking, *Why do I need to know the contract so well?* For me, it's like the Navy Seal who can take a gun apart and put it back together blindfolded. He understands that this piece of equipment keeps him alive in battle. Knowing how it works, how to clean it, fix it if it breaks, etc., could be the difference between life and death. Similarly, knowing the contract may keep it from busting and help you write or negotiate a deal. The contract is the most critical tool in our trade. Without it, there's no sale. No sale means no commission. No commission means you don't have a career.

Once you know the contract, create templates. For example, certain parts of the contract will always be the same. This creates

The contract is the most critical tool in our trade. Without it, there's no sale.

efficiency and keeps you from making mistakes. For example, when we're writing a contract on an investment property that's tenant occupied, we have written a purchase contract with pre-written verbiage in our Additional Provisions field that discusses when lease agreements should be turned in. It also states how deposits, pro-rated rents, etc., are to be given to the buyer. Our contract already has this in it, but it's often missed because many agents haven't read it. We got tired of pointing this out and arguing with brokers about it, so we created a template and addendum that goes with it. Now we don't have that problem.

Do you work with a particular type of client for which a template would help? Put it together and share it with your broker to ensure it meets all guidelines.

Read the contract and create templates. There isn't a lot to it. But it's critically important. You can do all the work mentioned in the previous chapters of this book and make zero dollars if you fail at the contract portion.

The Good

One of my agents came to me with a problem with her client, who wanted out of her contract. She had written a contract on a multi-million-dollar property for a client who lived in California. She was looking for an Oklahoma property since her family lived here. They found a house that "she loved and was perfect." In the contract, the agent had put in 5 percent earnest money, which was a considerable amount because of the sales price. During the inspection period, she started to have some minor second thoughts. She started wondering what else might be on the market that she could see. Like the yes people of Hollywood films, her assistant encouraged it.

"You should look at more homes."

"Looking at homes is so much fun."

"You can do what you want. You're the one with the money."

As my agent relayed the whole story to me, she said, "Since it's during the inspection period, she can bust and get her earnest money back, right?"

"Actually, no," I told her. "The new construction process doesn't have the same language around the inspection process as a standard purchase contract. Technically, the spirit of the regular contract doesn't either; it's just how so many agents and buyers view it. The new construction process states the buyer must submit a request for repairs or items that don't meet plans, guidelines, etc., and the builder has the right to make such repairs. The contract can be voided only if the builder refuses to do the requested repairs."

I then pulled up the contract and showed it to her.

"I've read this contract so many times, and I never noticed that," she said.

She then took it to her buyer and told her she could release the contract but would forfeit her earnest money. She decided that her whim of looking at other properties wasn't worth it. At which time her assistant began to tell her . . .

"This house is so perfect for you."

"You're going to love staying here when you're in Oklahoma."

"I'm so glad you found it."

I might be making that part up, but I'm sure it happened.

The Bad

"I made a mistake."

Not exactly what you want to hear from an agent, but taking ownership of a mistake and bringing it to my attention before it blows up goes a long way.

She'd just had a quick close on a property. The property had a tenant, and she'd completely forgotten about the deposit transfer and prorated rent at closing. When she called the other agent, the agent said, "He's keeping the deposit and rents because of the price he sold the property for."

She was sitting across from me and said, "I forgot to put it in the contract."

"You don't need to," I answered. "It's already in the contract."

I showed her where it was, and with a smile, she felt she had what she needed to get her client what was due.

After a lot of back and forth between her and the other agent, me, and the broker (who also didn't know it was in the contract) and the final threat of getting the State of Oklahoma involved for the seller violating Oklahoma's Landlord Tenant Act, the seller finally relinquished the deposit, but not the prorated rents.

This experience caused me to create the addendum template for properties with tenants that I mentioned earlier. Too many agents didn't know the contract, and we had to create an addendum to highlight what was already in the contract. I want to say that we've never had this problem again, but unfortunately, it seems that every time we don't use the addendum, we have to argue about the same things.

PART 4

PLAY NICE WITH OTHERS

22

YOU CAN'T DO THIS ALONE

There are many vendors and industry professionals you'll be working with in your real estate career, such as lenders, title reps, inspectors, appraisers, handymen, tradesmen, and many others. These folks can make or break a transaction, assist or work against you, grow your business, or pull from it.

Knowing how to play nice with these groups of professionals is one of the keys to our success and can be a vital component of your success. Growing and nurturing these relationships will bear fruit when it's needed most—when you need a lender to do a "hero deal" (that's when they close a deal in eight days from contract to close), or you need a contractor to drop everything and take care of a water leak the day of closing, or you ask a title rep to close on a Saturday to get a buyer into a property because they have nowhere to live. I can go on and on with examples of how respecting, growing, and nurturing vendor relationships has benefited my team, me, and, more importantly, our clients.

> Knowing how to play nice with these groups of professionals is one of the keys to our success and can be a vital component of your success.

I will go against the grain with my following statement. I stand against what is often taught, bragged about, and encouraged amongst agents, saying, "Never pay to play with your vendors." What do I mean by that? If you have an agreement with a vendor where they pay you or offer some benefit to you in return for working with them, they've paid, and you have to play. You've been bought.

Yes, RESPA has rules, regulations, and laws about how we all work together and support each other in our respected industry, but that's just how it's supposed to be done if it's done. But could there be a better way to nurture and be rewarded from a vendor relationship other than a monetary reward?

Tara and I were at a conference in Dallas, and we sat in the front row and listened to a leader of one of the most successful teams in the nation at the time. She talked about how her lender pays $6,000 monthly for different kinds of marketing for her. She said they'd found a way around marketing agreements that are no longer allowed, then went on to discuss how other vendors did the same for her team. For a moment, I thought, *Wow, I can outsource my expenses. That would be awesome.*

The next thought crashed that idea: *Then who owns who?*

Vendors love to work with agents because we have the clients most of the time. On average, most buyers start looking at houses way before they begin to talk to a lender. You don't buy home insurance before buying a home. You don't need a home inspector until you have a home to inspect. Agents tend to leverage their relationships with vendor partners because they're the gateway to the vendor getting clients. I'm not saying this shouldn't be done; you work hard to cultivate relationships. But what's the better way?

We've learned three things by not allowing our vendors to pay to play. First, we own our business. If a vendor partner doesn't care for the client, we move the business. That simple. If a lender pays $2,000 a month to advertise your profile on a third-party site, they don't need to do much more. They've bought your partnership, and you owe them. However, if they don't pay to play and want to keep your business, your clients always get front-of-the-line privileges.

We learned that a true partner will support your business by referring new clients back to you. The vendor partner keeps your business by supporting your business. Now, you may not get every referral or even zero referrals if they have a close relationship with another agent. If they respect your relationship with your clients, never interfere with it, *and* take care of your clients, then you should care about that. Your goal is to close the transaction.

We worked with a home inspector whose best friend was an agent for many years. We were okay with that because he was a damn good home inspector. Our clients always felt comfortable and were well taken care of. He held many transactions together by how he did his job, which was worth much more than a referral now and again. I'd rather have a vendor partner save five transactions than refer one client.

Third, we have the right to ask when we need a favor. We worked with a title company for many years. The president gave me his card one day with his personal cell phone number and said, "If you ever need anything, call me."

"Don't give this to me if you don't expect me to call," I said. "If I need something, it will be for a client and not me, but if I call, it will probably be a big ask."

"I know it will be for a client. You never ask for anything for yourself. That's why I'm giving it to you."

I had his number for almost a year before I called. We had a client who needed the help only a title company could do. Everyone on a local level told me no regarding what I needed. Without a yes, the transaction would fall apart in a bad way. So, I called the number on the card, made a request, and he approved and took care of it. Ultimately, everything worked out for all parties involved, including the title company. The client who was helped has referred so many people to our team since then because he was so appreciative and couldn't believe we pulled off this miracle for him.

Building Relationships with Vendor Partners

We'll explore some essential tips for building rapport among the various partners, but first, I want to share are few things that may help you.

Lunch is for rapport building; coffee or happy hour is for talking business. I've had too many unproductive or painful lunch experiences. It's hard to talk business and move a conversation from point A to point B when you're constantly interrupted by restaurant staff. *Can I get you water? Let me tell you about our specials. Here's your food. How is the food? Hi, I'm the manager. How is everything? Can I take your plate? Do you want dessert?* The interruptions come every five minutes. The flow is disrupted when you get to the important part of the conversation. Or worse, within the first ten minutes, you realize you won't be working with this person. Now you're on an uncomfortable blind date, wondering what else to discuss and who's picking up the tab. However, when you're just meeting for coffee or another beverage of choice, the meeting can end anytime. You have fewer interruptions and more time to ask questions to see if it's a good fit.

Once you begin to work together, if rapport building is the next step, then do that. I can tell you that the only dinners or lunches I have with vendor partners seem to be with lenders, title reps, or insurance agents. Everyone else is too busy.

Free is too good to be true. Everything needs to be a win-win scenario. It must make sense on their P&L as much as yours. Ask yourself why they're offering free leads, gift cards, etc. They should be good enough at what they do that it doesn't take a bribe to get you to work with them. My experience is that when a lender comes in offering leads, the leads end up being low quality, and the lender tends to struggle to put anyone under contract.

> Free is too good to be true. Everything needs to be a win-win scenario.

Working with Lenders

A great lender isn't the one who brings you donuts or pays for a broker's open house. A great lender has the same systems and processes for lead generation, lead follow-up, and standard operating procedures for moving a client from application to closing. So before referring a lender to your hard-earned leads for pre-qualification, do some research and ask some basic questions, such as:

"Tell me how you create business. What are your lead generation and lead follow-up processes?"

"When you receive an application or an inquiry, how long does it take to get them prequalified?"

"How do you determine what loan best meets a client's needs? By that, I mean, what questions do you ask the client?"

"How often do you update the client on the loan process once they're contracted to purchase?"

"What is your process for keeping your agent partners updated on the loan process?"

"Tell me about a difficult loan you were able to make happen. What was the situation, and how did you solve it?"

"How do you track leads, clients, referrals, etc., that you receive?"

"What's your process for keeping up with past clients?"

"When a client closes, how does your system notate that an agent referred a particular client?"

I could go on and on, but these few questions should get you through a twenty to thirty-minute interview with a lender.

If you're currently working with a lender, ask for a monthly report that details what referrals were received and where they are in the loan process. Lenders track their business, or at least they should, just like you should. If you're sending referrals to a lender and supporting their business, you want to ensure these referrals are A) being taken care of and B) staying with you.

At the beginning of your career or when you start working with a lender, you may be able to track every lead you send out. Think long term. Your lender partner is a strategic part of your business—not just in getting clients qualified and closing but also in lead cultivation. If you send someone who needs time to qualify, say three-plus months, you want to know the lender is checking in with them and keeping them as much as you're working to keep them in your world. The monthly report shows that they know where that lead was sourced as much as you do. Trust is vital in a business relationship. The monthly report helps maintain that trust.

Once under contract, ask when you'll receive updates about where the client is in the loan approval process. You should never find out a few days before closing that there's a problem or that the lender hasn't been working on it. We receive Friday updates from our lender partners for each referral, and once a month, I receive a spreadsheet with everyone we've sent over. Better yet, if we send someone over and they don't make an application, we also get notified of this. Request the same.

If the lender is local, meet the team. Go to their office and meet everyone. This is a rapport-building strategy that helps when a transaction gets tough. You aren't just some unhappy agent on the other end of the phone. They know your face and have met you in person, so they know you.

Markets fluctuate for lenders just as they do for real estate agents. When interest rates drop, homeowners refinance. When interest rates rise, that business begins to dwindle. If your lender is loyal to you, remain loyal to them. Don't be enticed away by a lender who specializes in refinances and now needs your business, so they offer to pay for every broker's open and promise free leads.

Finally, earn the lender's business. Don't expect the top lender in town to fall over you or drop an agent partner because you came into their lives. The business relationship goes both ways.

Working with Inspectors

Inspectors can make or break a deal. Just like with lenders, you need to form strategic relationships. Knowing how an inspector works with clients, responds to inspection results, and stands behind inspection reports are all critical to how they do business.

First and foremost, an inspector should never give their opinion of a property. Their job isn't to sway a client to purchase or walk away from a property based on the inspection report. No one needs to know how the inspector feels about a particular property. Like a doctor, you want the facts. A doctor wouldn't say, "Wow, you're fat." No, they may tell you that based on several factors, it's essential for you to reduce your weight because it's harming your body.

Second, ask about the home inspector insurance—what it covers during and after an inspection and for how long. This is important in case something is missed. For example, early in my career, an inspector forgot to check the stove on a vacant property. His insurance covered his oversight, and the client got a new stove. This is rare.

> Inspectors can make or break a deal. Just like with lenders, you need to form strategic relationships.

If you're working with a good inspector, they should have a system and process to ensure they don't miss anything.

Third, what does the inspection report look like? I despise inspection reports that have pre-filled information. For example, one of our agents began working with an inspector we had not yet vetted. A few days after closing, I got a call from a flustered agent because the client's washer drain line had backed up. I pulled up the inspection report before calling the client to see what the inspector wrote. It's not uncommon to receive a call after closing for something the client was told about but either thought it wasn't a big deal at the time or it wasn't an approved repair during the repair negotiation process.

I couldn't tell if the drain line had been inspected in this case. The vague phrasing described some general CYA (cover your ass) rhetoric to protect the inspector. I did a little research by looking at a few other inspections by the same home inspector, and each had the exact phrasing. We couldn't tell if the drain line had been inspected or missed.

Resolving this situation isn't essential, but avoiding a similar situation is. Inspection reports should be about that property. If there's no pool, there should not be a section that describes pools. Trust me, if things go sideways after a repair, the buyer will pick the inspection report apart, and referencing a pool that doesn't exist will add fuel to the fire.

Working with Title Companies

Oklahoma is a title company state, so I'm unfamiliar with states that close real estate transactions using attorneys. However, working with title companies is the same with any other vendor partner. Respect that they are there to create income for their company and themselves.

Asking the title rep to sponsor every broker's open house or golf tournament on your behalf isn't a sign of a good title company. Solving title defects, helping the client feel comfortable at closing, and staying a little late when something has to close are some traits that make a good title company. Ask yourself if you'd rather have the food at your broker's open house furnished by a title company or be able to call the title rep and say, "The buyer/seller is short on funds. Is there anything you can do?" If the rep dropped $1,000 to sponsor something for you, they will probably say no. It's time for you to contribute something to the relationship and drop your commission to close this one.

The benefits of working with vendor partners should always be for the clients and to close transactions. First, it's the right thing to do for the clients, and second, if transactions don't close, you don't make money. Respect that title companies exist to make money, too, so don't try to spend it all on lunches.

Working with Appraisers

Appraisers are not your enemies, so don't treat them like that. Technically, they aren't a vendor partner, but I feel they should be mentioned here because you must also play nice with them. Very few, if any, agents call an appraiser when the property meets or exceeds value to thank them for the great job they did. When an appraiser sees the value of some of the not-so-pronounced amenities of a property or finds suitable comparables for the house, we usually smile and move on with the transaction. But when an appraisal does not meet value, we call, gripe, fuss, and complain. I'm not saying that you should call and congratulate an appraiser. I'm merely stating that what they typically experience from an agent is getting into the house for the appraisal and then having that agent tell them why they don't know how to do their job when the appraisal is low.

Be proactive and helpful by giving the appraiser the tools to be successful. If the SQFT differs from the county records, inform the appraiser before the appraisal. If the property has upgrades, add-ons, a remodel, etc., gather the receipts/invoices from the seller and send them to the appraiser before the inspection. If you send them after the appraisal comes in low to raise the appraised value, it's like trying to move a line in the concrete. Good luck.

> Be proactive and helpful by giving the appraiser the tools to be successful.

Always meet the appraiser at the property. You typically don't need to stay the whole time, but meet them and introduce yourself. If you do this enough, they'll know you. I'm not saying that building rapport will mean you'll always have appraisals that come in at value, but it goes a long way with being professional and playing nice with others. If the value is low, you may get a call before the appraisal is submitted, asking you for any other comparables or amenities the appraiser might have missed.

If your market holds appraisal summits, go to them. Meet the appraisers, ask questions, learn how they assign value, and what they see in the market. If someone's job is to give an opinion of value, it's a good idea to learn how those opinions are formed.

Working with Insurance Agents

Without insurance, a lender will not close on a loan; at least, they're not supposed to. Yet, it's rare for an agent to be proactive about recommending an insurance agent. Real estate agents recommend lenders because we need to close transactions, and lenders recommend insurance because they need to close the transaction. The agent, the lender, and the insurance agent are the tripod of a transaction. If each works together, the client will benefit.

Most people sign up for insurance at one specific time and rarely change insurance agents or shop rates. We settle in and forget about it because it's not worth the hassle. But what if doing a little investigating could mean the difference between qualifying for a loan or not? Different policies and coverages have different rates. Let me say without going into too much detail: Many insurance agents can offer lower coverage that meets the lender's requirements and a lower premium that reduces the buyer's debt-to-income ratio to qualify for a loan. Once closed, the buyer can increase the coverage if they so desire. You never want a buyer to get into a house they can't afford or have subpar coverage. This is just for exceptional circumstances when the situation dictates.

I won't beat the drum again about working with vendor partners to get sponsorships. You get the point. A good partner will volunteer and ask to participate in broker open houses, brokerage events, etc. Be a good partner to them, and they'll return the favor. Insurance agents are no different.

Working with Contractors

Concerning contractors, I'm talking about handymen, plumbers, electricians, etc. These people get a property show-ready or make repairs when the contract dictates. Finding good contractors is hard; keeping good contractors is even more challenging.

A good contractor that's inexpensive won't work for you for long. Someone just starting the business often offers their services for less than everyone else. This is good for a while, but one day, they aren't going to answer your calls. Their business is growing, they've raised their rates to the standard, and you're left without a contractor. And it's typically when you need them the most. Be sure that they're good, and the price is fair. It needs to be a win-win for you and your client.

When you find a good contractor, be loyal. Send them enough business and never ask for anything for yourself—and when you need the hero deal, they'll come through. The hero deal could be when, on closing day, the waterline pops, and it needs to be fixed ASAP—along with the drywall, paint, etc. They come through for you and the seller. At the same time, they make the buyer feel comfortable to go through with the closing. Hero.

Be sure not to quote your contractors to death. Don't constantly ask them to quote a repair for which they get the work one out of ten times. Contractors must perform jobs to make money. And they don't usually make money on quotes. Do this enough times, and you'll finally hear a no and lose a good contractor.

Make sure the contractors get paid. This isn't your responsibility, but do your part by submitting invoices promptly. The contractor has the client's billing info, and the client knows they're responsible for payment.

In short, respect the contractor's business, and they'll take care of your business. When you ask for that favor, they'll know it's to save a transaction and support you.

Working with Everyone Else

If you haven't yet compiled a vendor list, now is the time to do it. Many real estate coaches will have you assemble a list for lead generation purposes and ask you to call contractors to say, "You take care of me, and I'll take care of you." Why would they? They just met you. Instead, create a list of contractors to help you and your clients close a transaction. Create a list of vendors that do the job right. If you want their referral business, show them you're worth the business. Here's a quick list you can start with:

- Lender(s)
- Home insurance agents
- Property managers (if you don't do it yourself)
- Bankers (different from the lender)
- Attorneys (from real estate to estate planning)
- Home inspector
- Pest inspector
- Handyman
- Painter
- Electrician
- Plumber
- Roofer
- Lawn care and maintenance
- Sprinkler technician
- Title reps
- Home warranty providers
- Carpet/flooring expert
- Cleaners
- Trash hauling company
- Movers

- Stagers
- Photographers/videographers

I'll end with this final note. You may not work with these vendors weekly or even monthly. That doesn't mean you shouldn't call and check in with them to see how their business is going. Let them know they're top of mind, and they may do the same for you.

The Good

Tara and I sat in a posh country club, lunching with a husband-and-wife mortgage team. Listening to their systems and processes, we were super impressed. So impressed we made notes on improving some of our standard operations procedures (SOPs).

Toward the end, I asked several strategic questions with an end game in mind.

Me: *"How many other agents do you work with?"*

Him: *"We work with most of the top agents in the market."*

Me: Oh, not going to give me a straight answer, *I thought.* *"You've told us about your marketing and previous client follow-up. So, how often do you have clients not currently working with an agent?"*

Him: *"Most of the time, our clients have already spoken with an agent, but occasionally, we have one or two a month."*

Me: *"Who do you typically refer them to, or how do you decide who to refer them to?"*

Him: *"We don't have a specific agent we refer because we want to be fair to all our partners. It depends on the client and finding the best agent that's the best match. We must protect our business as much as we need to support yours."*

Me: Damn, *I thought.* That's a good answer. I can respect that.

Tara and I left that meeting and started working with that lender. This was around 2008. As I write this story, we've consistently worked with that lender for the past fifteen years. Yes, we always have a second lender we work with, but the number of back-ups has changed more times than I can count. Our number one has remained number one because they are number one—the best in the business. Our clients are always taken care of and receive the best service; the company always does what it says it will.

That's not the end of this story. After about a year of working with them, I noticed they gave us one to two leads a month. At first, I was thankful, but I didn't think much of it. I figured we were a better fit than their other agent partners.

But when we received the ninth or tenth lead, I called and asked, "Hey, I noticed we receive a lot of referrals from you, and I'm very thankful. Can you tell me why?"

"You take care of the client," they said. "You keep up with them, and Tara typically finds them a home within a week or two. No one takes better care of our clients than you and Tara. Other agents take weeks or months, don't have a good follow-up with the client, or don't let us know where they are in the home-search process."

Referrals aside, I don't think our relationship with this couple, business or personal, would have developed if I'd asked them at that first lunch to pay to play. If I'd asked them to sponsor brokers' open houses, lunch and learns, or other things again and again, they may have done it. Still, I don't think we'd have received the referrals like we did, not to mention the other non-monetary benefits we've received through their friendship over the years. By respecting their business— their profit and loss—right from the beginning and over the years, they respected ours.

The Bad

If you've been an agent long enough, you will have your share of horror stories about vendors who weren't vetted. Here are a few snapshots of our experiences, some that have happened to my agents and some where we were bought into the situation or discovered later.

- The roof was put on without decking. I don't even know how this was possible. The shingles were floating and attached to the rafters in places.
- "I would never buy this house." I've heard this from multiple home inspectors, most of whom are no longer in the business.
- The house was in the middle of the city, but to save money on installing a sewer line to the city services (which required going under the road), the builder installed a septic tank and told no one. When the buyer went to sell, the home inspector discovered it. The cost to connect to the city sewer line was over $30,000. The house was only worth about $80,000 at the most. The city condemned the septic tank, and the owner was told the house couldn't be occupied until the sewer situation was fixed. The seller gave the house to the bank in foreclosure.
- A handyman electrified the shower when repairing the attic. The buyer was shocked (not too bad) while showering.
- The home inspector forgot he was filling the upstairs tub, and in mid-conversation, water started pouring out of the cam lights in the kitchen onto the buyer.
- The roofer went to the wrong house and removed all the shingles before the owner got home. This one didn't end up too bad. They got a new roof for free.

- The lawn care company was charging to mow the front and back yards but was only mowing the front. The backyard grass grew to roughly five feet high.
- The home inspector's license lapsed, and he didn't tell anyone. We found out from another home inspector in a passing conversation.
- To find a slab leak, the plumber made multiple holes in the floors throughout the property. He never fixed the holes or found the leak; he just left, and they never heard from him again.
- The home inspector never went into the attic to check the HVAC. The duct work had numerous holes and was disconnected throughout. But the attic was nice and cool!
- The roofer had vents, but not actual holes, to allow air to pass through the vents. The roof lasted only a few years from the hot summers, and insurance didn't cover replacement.
- The seller's handyman illegally tapped into the city gas line, bypassing the gas meter at the property. This wasn't discovered until some time later.
- A contractor sent us $7,000 in invoices that they had failed to collect for one reason or another over a year. They thought that since we referred the client to them, we should pay the invoices even though we had nothing to do with the repairs. No, we didn't pay the invoices.
- The title company missed an easement that showed an oil pipeline going through the lot. When the buyer had a storm shelter installed, they struck oil.
- The seller found a tile worker on Craigslist who was cheaper than the ones I recommended. After this work, the kitchen and bathrooms had to be gutted, and they had to start over, doubling the cost of materials.

- The lender requested a one-week extension, and the buyer and seller agreed. The lender asked for another extension, this time for two weeks. The buyer and seller agreed again. Now, three weeks past the closing date, my agent got me involved because the sellers were getting frustrated. I called the lender and asked when we would have a clear to close. His response was, "Oh, this isn't going to close. The buyer can't get qualified. I knew this three weeks ago."

"Then why have we been extending?" I asked.

"I didn't want to tell the buyer that I forgot to look at his file until the day of closing," he said

"Why didn't you tell us?" I asked.

"I didn't have to," he answered.

"I want to be super pissed, but you've been so honest right now that I don't know what to say."

PART 5

TIME AND MONEY

23

PROTECT YOUR TIME

The standard joke about starting your own business is that you did it to control your schedule, but now you work 24/7, and your clients control it for you. First, let me say there's no such thing as work and personal life balance. If you think you're going to achieve it, good luck. I've found that there's a constant shifting between work and personal life, and you must manage the flow. Too much work and you lose your family. Too much personal time and you lose your business.

After twenty-two years, a good friend is getting ready to retire from the Navy. He told me he's been to so many retirement parties where the retiring sailor, with tears in his eyes, looked over at his wife and kids and said, "You will be a priority for me now. I know I haven't put you first over the years, but now I will."

"What bullshit," my friend said. "The first time I heard someone say that, I thought, *Why would your family want you now? Oh, now that you can't be in the Navy anymore, now that you have to retire, now you have time for your family.* I decided then that wouldn't be me. I gave my all, but I never let my family come second."

In case you're wondering what type of sailor my friend is, he's one of the youngest Master Chiefs in the history of the Navy. Ask his wife or kids; they'll tell you they never felt second place. Even when he was on six to twelve-month deployments. He didn't get to control his schedule. The government did that for him, but he still found ways to make his family feel like they were his priority.

You get to control your schedule; you do. You must learn to schedule your time to avoid burnout for you, your family, or your friends. And a calendar is your key.

> You get to control your schedule; you do. You must learn to schedule your time to avoid burnout for you, your family, or your friends.

Step one to controlling your time is to put everything into that calendar. I'm not talking about time blocking; that's next-level time control. I am merely telling you to put everything into a schedule, including personal events. Step two is to treat anything in your calendar as an appointment. Clients don't know if your appointment is closing with a client or lunch with your kids. You're setting up the time with the seller to see the property, so script the conversation in a way that doesn't leave room for questions. Here are some examples of what I mean:

"I have a 1:00 p.m. appointment today. Are you available at noon or 2:30 p.m.?"

"I can get us into the property at 4:00 p.m. today. Does that work?"

"The property is occupied, so they'll need some notice. Does 5:00 p.m. work for you?"

"Tuesday, I am in appointments until 2:00 p.m. Can we meet that afternoon or evening?"

This works with clients who love to call or text whenever a question or thought comes to mind. An agent I coached had a client who "demanded that he respond right away, or he would get angry."

My response was, "The next time he texts you, respond with, 'I'm tied up in an appointment 'til 12:30. I can text you as soon as I'm out.' If it's after 12:30, give him another time you're available, like 4:30 p.m. And then make sure you text him back at that time."

Guess what? He did this, and the client wasn't angry at all. The client's response was, "Great. Talk to you then."

If you value your time, your clients will, too. No one expects a doctor or an attorney to respond immediately, but they do expect them to respond. If you're good at what you do, and your clients think you're good at what you do, they'll assume you have other clients. I didn't say, "I'm showing other homes until 2:00 p.m., but I'll be free afterward." No need to say you're with someone else. Just say you have an appointment. This is also true for personal appointments—no need to share the specifics. You're in an appointment, period.

Professional Time

Busy work is just that, busy work. You'll have to learn the difference between busy work and actual work that produces or maintains income.

An agent I coach came to me super frustrated and said, "All I do is work, like twelve to fourteen hours a day."

"Really? Okay," I said. "Before we can streamline your activities, let's figure out what you do daily. When you're engaged in an income-producing or income-maintenance activity for the next two weeks, I want you to write down how much time you spent doing it and what you're doing."

Two weeks later, we met again, and this time, he had a smile on his face.

"So tell me about the time spent working the last two weeks," I began.

"Well, it turns out I'm only working twenty to twenty-five hours a week," he said. "The rest of the time, I'm just wasting time."

This agent was twenty then and made about $150,000 a year, working twenty to twenty-five hours a week. Too often, we get distracted by busy or unproductive work and think we're doing real estate. No, we're just wasting time and calling it real estate. Business lunches that go nowhere, meetings that produce no tangible results, and classes where you don't implement any actual items are all a waste of time. Respect your time.

> Too often, we get distracted by busy or unproductive work and think we're doing real estate.

Another way to control your time is to pick up and call. Be proactive. You can't put a task away until it's completed. Waiting for an email response is a waste of time. So, make the call. It takes less time and gets the results you need.

Client Time

Most people are indecisive. Ask ten people if they're indecisive, and they'll likely say, "Yes and no. Sometimes I am, and sometimes I'm not, so maybe I am. I'm not sure." You can help your clients with their time by giving them options. If you give them the infinite possibilities of "What's the best time to meet?" most will have to "get back to you" to figure out the best time to meet. Give them two times and let them pick one. If those times don't work, give them one more. If that time doesn't work, ask, "What time does work?"

Second, if possible, wear your clients out when looking at houses. By that, I mean schedule as many as you can to view. You do this every day; it's your job.

But they are looking at properties in addition to their already full life. If you show them enough houses at a time, they'll find the one that fits most of their needs and wants. If you look at one or two houses at a time, be prepared to work with them for weeks or months.

You must also respect your clients' time. Never be late for an appointment. We already discussed this in Part 3: Keep It Professional. But it's worth repeating. Be on time.

24

MONEY

A poor agent is a poor agent. If you're an agent driven by your need for money, at the end of the transaction, you'll struggle to make decisions that truly benefit the client if they jeopardize the transaction. It isn't easy to guide clients to make a good decision that benefits them when you desperately need that commission.

Mythical, Magical Money

To be a great agent, you must understand that no transaction is guaranteed. The commission check promised is mythical, magical money until that check is handed to you when a transaction has closed.

Whether you sell only a few properties a year or many more than that, learning to manage your business and personal finances must become a priority. That's what this chapter is about, and it includes teaching you the basics of real estate investing. Not investing in real estate is like being a chef who doesn't eat his food.

Let's go back to mythical, magical money for just a second. All commission checks are mythical, magical money until the check is in hand. Once it's in hand, you get to spend it. That's when your plan to spend it goes into play. By learning to have a business budget, any profit and loss statement (it does not have to be complicated), a weekly time to review, and a few other best practices, you'll avoid the dreaded "I need this to close; I need the money" crisis.

> Whether you sell only a few properties a year or many more than that, learning to manage your business and personal finances must become a priority.

I received a surreal phone call in my first year of real estate. The transaction was a few days from closing. It was a Tuesday, and the closing was scheduled for Friday. The seller and buyer disagreed about a repair item. I believe the transaction needed to be pushed or not close at all. No deal is better than a bad deal. I mentioned this to the other agent and said, "Look, this is a rough deal. I don't think it benefits either of our clients." My voice was calm and rational.

The response on the other side of the phone was not calm and far from rational. It was the first time I'd heard a real estate agent say, "No, this has to close. I need the money." It was the first time but, unfortunately, not the last time.

I was okay with the transaction not closing. I didn't need the commission check to feed my family or pay my bills. From her demanding tone, I can only assume this agent's finances weren't in order. So much so that getting her commission check was more important than serving her client.

Of course, when starting real estate, you may not have money in the bank to carry you through. That's why you must play the "next" game. Once the client is under contract, everything you do is income maintenance. When you're working with a new client, everything is income production. Too many agents put a contract under and focus on closing that transaction. Nothing else. Yes, some activities need to happen during the contract period, but these activities don't take all day every day. So do what must be done, and then get out there and put more clients under contract. Get more homes sold.

I didn't think much about the income side of things when I first started. I just focused on how many transactions my wife and I could put under contract. If we put "more rounds down range," we had a better chance of hitting the target. Initially, it was about selling as many houses as possible to ensure we'd be okay if a transaction didn't close. During my first year, we closed just under eighty transactions. This was all Tara, with me working as her assistant for the second part of the year. Then 2008 came, and the housing market crashed. We closed over eighty transactions that year, too. When the market went down, we exceeded the year before. We ignored what people were saying about the market, and we just kept working on transactions.

Find Your Baseline

The first thing you need to do is find your baseline. This is the minimum amount of money you need monthly to live. I'm talking the bare minimum: house, car, insurance, utilities, bills, and basic food. I mean basic food to live. We're talking about what it takes to live without eating out, fine dining, T-bone steaks, caviar, sushi, vacations, nights out at the movies, etc. The very bare minimum amount you need to live on. Once you have that number, you know what amount to use to create a budget, what excess you need to put into savings to offset months below the baseline, and anything left over to pay off debt.

Let me ask you a question. How much money could you save if you lived on the bare minimum for three to six months? How much debt could you possibly pay off? We go through this exercise yearly with our team during our goal-planning retreats. This past year, a new couple who joined our team was amazed. They made three times their baseline yet said they "had no money." They had savings but not what they could have.

> How much money could you save if you lived on the bare minimum for three to six months?

Knowing your baseline allows you to gain perspective about what you spend. Agents work on commission, so some months are better than others. Your baseline lets you know that if you need a minimum of $5,500 a month to live and make $7,000 in one month, then you can save $1,500 that month. Maybe the next month, you make $10,000, so you save $4,500, and the next month you make $8,500, adding another $3,000 to savings. You now have $9,000 in savings in three months—or you paid off $9,000 in debt. These numbers reflect your ability to make less than $100,000 annually. Dave Ramsey said it best when he said, "You have to live like no one else if you want to live like no one else." Whether you like him or not, that's a good quote.

After you figure out your baseline, you can think about your "better life." This is when you add in going to the movies once or twice a month or getting that T-bone steak at the grocery store. You're adding in some essential luxuries. You're controlling that additional income. How much do you need to make to live a better life and pay off your debt?

After the better life comes the "luxury life." This is where you buy a new car, go on those extra vacations, maybe buy a boat. I don't have a boat, but every time I teach this to a group, at least half the people say they want to buy a boat. What does the luxury life cost you each month? How much do you need to earn to elevate your life to the luxury level? Some of you are already living the luxury life on a better life income—or worse, a baseline income. So, your debt continues to rise, or you're one bad month away from financial ruin. If you do this exercise, you know exactly what you need to earn to live this lifestyle, so you may need to take a step back to achieve it.

Now it's time to dream a little with the "dream life" income. What does living your dream life look like? What vacations do you take? What second home(s) do you own? What does a dream life look like to you? What legacy are you leaving behind? My dream life is leaving behind a legacy where my great, great grandkids still talk about Tara and me. This goes beyond financial.

I'll end with this. If you're hung up on, "Oh, it's all about material things," then you've missed the point. I find those who criticize others about their material things are typically the ones who are hung up on material things. If you make $45,000 a year, how much can you truly give to help others, including your time? If you make $450,000 a year, how much could you give? What about $4,500,000 a year? You cannot give what you do not have.

Track Your Money

So, how much do you have? It's time to start tracking your money if you haven't already. If you figured out your baseline, you know how much your life costs. What about your business life? Where's the money going? And does it provide a return? A profit and loss statement to track income and expenses will help you make better decisions. Never decide by saying, "It's just selling one more house." The one more house profit and loss plan will put you in debt before you know it.

Each week, we review every dollar that came in and every expense. From that, we know what's creating a return and what's only an expense. It wasn't always like this. Before we had a true P&L or had these weekly meetings, we were living in the excess of overflow. We were making so much that we had plenty to spend. *Why worry or think about it too much? All is good!* Luckily, our accountant showed us how we made much more money as a company, but our take-home was much less because our expenses were way out of control. We were losing so slowly we thought we were winning. Fortunately, the market stayed good the following year, allowing us to right the ship before the ship sank. Get caught over-spending and living too good a life when the market shifts, and you may find yourself in financial ruin. Trust me; I've met plenty of agents who find themselves out of the business and trying to dig their way out of debt.

> It's time to start tracking your money if you haven't already.

You don't need anything fancy to track your finances in the beginning. A simple spreadsheet with all your business expenses each month will work. It's what we used at first. Just put them all on there. Write down what the item is and what the monthly expense is. Don't forget any quarterly or yearly items, such as dues or state fees. From this, you can see what you need each month, by the month, to do business. This is your business baseline, much like your personal baseline.

As commission checks come in, you can see what business debt needs to be paid before you can pay yourself. As you progress and your business grows, you can start working with an accountant or a program such as Quickbooks®.

Begin with the basics. As you become more proficient in tracking your expenses, you'll naturally seek and develop more sophisticated ways of running your business that will reduce time, track dollars spent, and much more.

Invest Your Money

Now it's time to talk about what to do with your extra cash as you better control your expenses. It's time for you to create some additional income outside of simply selling houses and to create additional income by personally buying and selling houses. Too many agents don't realize they are *in* real estate; they don't just need *to do* it. You should know a good deal when you see one, and you'll see deals before the public does.

> It's time for you to create some additional income outside of simply selling houses and to create additional income by personally buying and selling houses.

Let me give you an example. A property was listed online—very poorly, I might add. Yes, the flooring was not great, and the master bathroom had pink tile from floor to ceiling, but it hadn't sold because it wasn't showing. The property had abysmal marketing, and the seller reduced the price a few times as it sat. So, we put in a slightly more aggressive offer than the list price. The seller accepted. We put together a basic remodel plan/ budget and calculated the possible list price and return we would make. It was a good number. But before we began the work, we had the house cleaned, professionally photographed and put it on the market for $30,000 more than the original list price. It sold in three weeks. Even more crazy was that agents told us what a fabulous remodel we did.

Of course, that was a rare case, but my point is that because we knew the market and were looking for deals for ourselves, we, were ready to take advantage of one when it came along. The significant investment deals you pass on to your clients should not fit how you want to invest.

Hopefully, this will whet your appetite for what's possible and what you can and should be doing. If you want to start investing, plenty of great books explore in-depth real estate investing. For a list of books, go to LevinsonEDU.com.

25

YOU'RE NOT THE FIRST AGENT

Agents rarely attend trainings other than those required for continuing education to keep their licenses. Even fewer have a mentor or coach in the business. I recommend a more involved approach.

Keep Educating Yourself

You're reading this book, so good on you to continue your education. Never stop improving your knowledge. And yet, going to a bunch of classes, reading a bunch of books, and getting a bunch of certifications won't make you successful in real estate. You must implement what you learn to gain from all that education. I make it a point to choose at least one thing to implement, improve, or stop doing from every class I take or book I read.

I'm always reading at least one real estate or business book, whether it's about sales, investing, or business principles. I want to learn from others before I have to experience the hardships someone else has already endured and overcome. That's why I read the book of Job in the Bible every year. *I got it, God,* I think. *No need to teach me directly what Job learned.* No need to reinvent the wheel in real estate either. Find someone who has a great wheel and find out what they did.

Find a Coach/Mentor

Everyone should have a mentor or guide in real estate. Sales have been around for thousands of years. The current basic ways of conducting real estate sales have existed for decades. Why travel the path without a guide? Find a mentor or coach. The purpose of a coach/mentor is to have a resource outside your professional sphere who can answer your questions and guide you, someone who has that 30,000-foot view of your business and the market as a whole, someone who can guide you regarding what you're doing and where you're going with your career.

> The purpose of a coach/mentor is to have a resource outside your professional sphere who can answer your questions and guide you ...

A mentor doesn't have to be someone you pay or even know. It can simply mean following someone else's direction, principles, and teachings. For example, David Goggins is one of Tara's mentors right now. She's never met David Goggins and may never meet him. But she reads and rereads his books, listens to podcasts where he's featured, follows him on social media, etc. If he recommends a book, she reads it. She just finished a book on elk hunting because David recommended it. She has zero plans to elk hunt, even though I keep teasing her that we're going next year to put her skills to the test. But her "mentor" recommended it, and she read it. And guess what? She learned a lot from it (the book goes beyond elk hunting). If you're curious, the book is called *Endure: How to Work Hard, Outlast, and Keep Hammering* by Cameron Hanes. It's a pretty badass book.

When your budget allows, get a real estate coach. I'd been in real estate for almost four years before I got a coach. Honestly, I didn't even know they existed. I was pretty content with just making up stuff as I went. Yes, sometimes I'd find the right way, and sometimes I spent a lot of marketing dollars on something that didn't bring a return on my investment. But in 2010, when Tara and I made a brokerage switch, we were assigned a free coach for two weeks as an intro to coaching. We quickly learned the benefit of having a trusted advisor, someone with an outside perspective on our business, and someone to hold us accountable each week to do what we said we would. We worked with that coach for over twelve years. Our business wouldn't be where it is today without that outside counsel, harsh feedback when we needed it, strong mentoring when it was called for, and willful guidance. When we had an idea or roadblock, he was there to ask us the questions we weren't asking ourselves.

Today, I coach my agents to assist in their growth. I don't offer it; my agents have to request it. And it comes with stipulations. First, we'll only focus on what they want to develop, so they need to know what that is. We explore that in the first meeting. Second, there's an expectation that they'll complete the homework. Homework is what they need to implement based on what they want. If we meet a couple of times and they haven't done the work, we stop meeting until they do. Coaching without implementation is a waste. If and when you get a coach, be sure they hold you accountable.

The Good

It was good to be prepared for a bad time. It was March of 2020. Most of the United States was shut down in response to the spread of COVID-19. In Oklahoma, the governor had not yet deemed real estate agents essential, so Tara and I, like most agents in the United States, were told we couldn't work.

The foreseeable future, in that moment, was unknown. Tara and I live on five acres between Oklahoma City and Edmond, Oklahoma. It was about 9:30 at night, and we were in our hot tub discussing what was happening in the world, both locally and abroad, and how it could affect our family, friends, and real estate team. We felt good. We had a freezer full of food; coincidently, a month or so earlier, we had over-ordered toilet paper from Amazon, our house was paid off, and we had zero dollars in personal debt and enough savings for a minimum of six months if no other income was generated.

I share this because I want to ask you, "Were you prepared?" Are you prepared right now? If you suddenly couldn't work, are you financially sound enough to weather that storm? How long could you maintain your lifestyle without going further in debt? How long could you last financially without a closing or a paycheck?

To this day, I'm thankful that Tara and I began paying off our debt way before March 2020. I'm thankful that we had personal and business savings to continue to pay our support staff for a time if no income was created.

Thankfully, we were again able to work, and the market saw unprecedented highs. Markets will constantly shift. You may have months and years when you make a lot of money. And you may have months and years when you make very little money. Are you prepared for both? Are you prepared to make the right financial decisions when you're in times of feast so you can live well during times of famine?

Though COVID wasn't a good time for many, I tell this story because it was good that we were prepared. My hope for you is that you'll be prepared to weather any market shifts the future may bring.

The Bad

It was supposed to be a good day. We had two closings: for one, we had both sides of the transaction, and for the other, we had the buyer. This was roughly 2009. The average gross commission was around $3,700 based on our average sales price. We were going to make a little over $11,000 that day. Our sellers were military and pre-signed the Friday prior, then moved to their new duty station over the weekend. It was a quick closing, and the title company was still putting in the final numbers. The buyers weren't scheduled to go in until that afternoon to sign and consummate the transaction. At about 9:30 a.m., I received a call from the title company.

"The sellers had a second loan on the house. Did you know that?"

"Uhh, no, they never mentioned it. When we calculated the net to the seller, they said there was only one loan. No other liens on the property."

"Well, they do, and it has them bringing money to closing."

"How much?"

When I heard the number, I knew what was going on. It was roughly the amount we were going to make in commission.

"Let me call you back," I said.

I immediately called the seller, and after a brief conversation, the seller said, "Yup, we're not bringing money to closing. Either you figure it out, or we're not closing."

We had a problem. On one hand, the seller's problem wasn't our problem. On the other hand, we brought the buyers to the house; they trusted us, and if it didn't close, they had nowhere to live. All their stuff was on a moving truck waiting to enter the house. So, we let go of the commission to take care of the buyer and closed the transaction. I also may or may not have hired a shaman to put a curse on those sellers. Just saying.

I received another call after my call to the title company to cut our commission. It was from a lender saying the buyer on our other transaction could no longer qualify. I honestly don't even remember why. At that point, I was in a daze and wondered why I bothered putting on a tie that morning.

And there you have it. In less than two hours, $11,000 disappeared. Today, based on average sales prices, it would be the equivalent of nearly $30,000. That's the day I realized that all money is mythical, magical money until it's in your hands.

AFTERWORD

Our practical journey has come to an end. I've attempted to impart practical, actionable ways to create business, told you what to do with a lead when you get one, advised how to keep it professional, and imparted a few other things along the way.

I hope you'll take this information and grow your business, and one day, you'll go from practical to overflow. That you will have a year when you make over a million dollars in commissions. That you become that millionaire real estate agent.

Between now and then, continue to do the simple things. Be repetitive. Success is boring. Success is doing the same actionable items every day. Success is repeating the same scripts over and over again. What we do isn't complicated; it's repetitive. It's showing up every day and doing the same things. Sometimes, that's not sexy, but it is practical. And practical is about doing. So be practical and do the work.

ABOUT THE AUTHOR

Peter Levinson's journey began in the United States Marine Corps, where he served as Sergeant Levinson for five years. From working on KC-130 aircraft to carrying heavy packs and driving boats, Peter experienced diverse challenges that prepared him for the demanding nature of the business world.

Following his honorable discharge, Peter embarked on a new chapter in his life and transitioned into the business sector. He joined Circuit City as a salesperson and quickly rose through the ranks, becoming a store manager within a few years. From there, he transitioned to Best Buy as a regional marketing manager before moving into real estate.

Peter then ventured into the real estate industry. He joined Coldwell Banker Realty as a realtor and specialized in listing and marketing homes and assisting home buyers. In 2010, Peter took a significant step in his career by becoming the branch office broker for Levinson Real Estate Team/Keller Williams Central Oklahoma. Specializing in residential sales, luxury properties, builders, relocation, military PCS, and investment properties, his expertise expanded rapidly. His team employed a large administration staff, including marketing, processing, and sales specialists, providing comprehensive client support.

In 2019, he became the branch office broker for Levinson Real Estate Team with eXp and OKC Management. Operating as a unified team, the brokerage offers full-service real estate solutions to clients. Peter and his team stand out in the industry by leveraging advanced marketing techniques and a client-centered approach.

Peter earned a bachelor's degree in business from the University of Phoenix in 2007. Later, he pursued a master's degree in pastoral studies from Southwestern Christian University between 2010 and 2012.

Peter Levinson's journey from military service to the real estate industry is a testament to his dedication, resilience, and passion for facilitating growth in people's lives. With a career spanning over two decades, Peter's expertise, leadership, and commitment to client success have established him as a trusted figure in the Oklahoma City Metropolitan Area. Whether assisting clients in buying or selling properties, mentoring his team, or employing advanced marketing strategies, his contributions to the real estate landscape continue to make a lasting impact. Through his work, he helps clients achieve their real estate goals and inspires personal growth, transformation, and success.